Understanding Educational Leadership
People, power and culture

Hugh Busher

Open University Press

Open University Press
McGraw-Hill Education
McGraw-Hill House
Shoppenhangers Road
Maidenhead
Berkshire
England
SL6 2QL

email: enquiries@openup.co.uk
world wide web: www.openup.co.uk

and Two Penn Plaza, New York, NY 1012–2289 USA

First published 2006

Copyright © Hugh Busher 2006

A catalogue record of this book is available from the British Library

ISBN-10: 0 335 21717 6 (pb)   0 335 21718 4 (hb)
ISBN-13: 978 0 335 21717 5 (pb)   978 0 335 21718 2 (hb)

Library of Congress Cataloging-in-Publication Data
CIP data applied for

1004766701

Typeset by BookEns Ltd, Royston, Herts.
Printed in Poland by OZ Graf. S.A.
www.polskabook.pl

Contents

List of figures, tables and vignettes

Figures

Tables

Vignettes

Preface

This book began as part of a modernist project to consider and refine how schools could be developed to create positive cultures that would foster successful learning through the support of exciting teaching and enthusiastic teachers. However, fascination with the political processes of bringing about change in schools, and the chance remark of a teacher, once a student and then a co-researcher of the author – oh, the poli-tics of this place! – have led to the project taking on a distinctly critical and post-structuralist hue that not only questions the ways in which power flows around schools but also the values attached to it by people trying to access and use it to achieve their agenda, whether for what they claim are altruistic purposes or for reasonable self-interest.

This focus on power, its uses and projection and the values and purposes for which it is used, stands at the core of this book as it attempts to balance modernist and critical agenda by considering how leaders at all levels in schools – from the most senior manager to the classroom teacher – negotiate and work with their colleagues, students and their parents and carers, as well as with external agencies and the local social communities in which a school's students live, to construct, sustain and improve successful learning and promote a sense of community among the students and staff who are members of a school. The book's conceptual framework is drawn from a literature on the nature of leadership, especially distributed and teacher leadership, education management, school improvement and the construction of collaborative work groups, and on critical perspectives of the micro-political processes of change and the relationship of people in school communities or organizations to their social, economic and policy contexts.

Hugh Busher

1 Considering schools as organizations and communities

Making sense of schools from different perspectives

Schools as institutions have many features in common with other institutions – as well as some crucial differences. The features that are similar might be described as follows:

- A structure of formal roles or 'statuses', arranged into a social hierarchy into which expectations regarding appropriate behaviour ('role performance') are built.
- A collection of individual human beings whose behaviour is related to a greater or lesser extent to the roles they play in the same structure.
- Between the formal structures and the individuals are what might be called informal or micro-political structures and processes characterized more by coalitions than by departments, by strategies rather than rules, by influence rather than power and by knowledge rather than status (Hoyle 1982).
- A set of more or less related aims, values, beliefs, attitudes and ideas manifested through rituals, rules and language and through the perspectives and positions that individuals adopt to the institution and other individuals and which form the culture of the institution and the subcultures of its departments.
- A set of interactions of varying intensity and continuity between members of the institution and the individuals and groups which, taken collectively, constitute its environment.

(Ribbins 1985)

The crucial differences relate to the participants in schools the majority of whom, in England and Wales, are under the age of adulthood and are required by central government to attend them between the ages of 5 years and 16 years. Consequently most people attend the same institution and work with the same people for many years at a time and are not free to leave when they want to. A further important difference is that the leaders and managers of a school are adult staff while the majority of the other participants, the workers of the school who do the work of constructing knowledge (Starratt 1999), are children. This raises major questions about what are appropriate styles of social relationships between staff and students, and between staff when visible to the students. It also inhibits a range of social interactions that, in other organizations, might break down barriers between people of different formal status.

Yet another difference is that the outcomes of schools are multifaceted and only some are relatively easy to measure. Although central government in England and Wales in the early twenty-first century set great store by measuring the academic attainment of school pupils, arguably it is the other outcomes – people's personal, social, physical, aesthetic and moral developments – that are more important and of greater consequence to the shaping of their adult lives, although academic attainment constrains entry to the adult labour market. A further difference is the blurred nature of a school's organizational boundaries. These semi-permeable membranes allow for osmosis between a school and the local social and business communities in which state schools are deeply embedded. As Demie (2004) has argued, the more closely school staff work with parents, especially in areas of social disadvantage where many children are disaffected, the more the achievement of students improves.

On account of these differences schools seem to carry many of the hallmarks of communities, as Sergiovanni (1994) argues. They are made up of people who expect to be part of them for many years, staff as well as students. Although people attend for instrumental reasons (having a job, learning subject knowledge), many students indicate that their main reasons for attending are to enjoy being with and sharing activities with their friends (Beresford 2003). Teachers, too, value the social side of being in school and working alongside colleagues who are perceived as friends. Authentic relationships of respect and understanding are closely allied to instrumental success in learning and teaching (Hopkins *et al.* 1997b). Contractually based definitions of role and function only partially describe teachers' working lives as they construct them and normally provide only a weak base for their authority. This projection of formal power is more strongly founded on interpersonal skills, qualities and relationships. Schools are purposeful communities primarily focused on people's personal and social development, although legislation since the late 1980s in England and Wales has focused school outcomes on the targeted academic performance of students in order to better prepare them for entering the local and national labour market at 16 years old.

Many of these characteristics make schools similar to custodial institutions, like prisons (Foucault 1977) – for example, the strongly asymmetrical relationships that exist between staff and students as well as the power that staff wield to define what might be considered socially acceptable and unacceptable behaviours. Some of the behaviours which staff sanction or prescribe would be considered largely unacceptable in organizations in which all members were adults, unless perhaps in the armed forces, the police or prisons. Students are not treated as equal members of the community with adult staff when formally shaping the development of the community, its culture and its purposes and rules of engagement and activity. Indeed attempts by students to engage in this debate are often regarded with hostility by staff and usually result in students being punished in various ways. Schools' apparent major purpose of preparing students to be docile participants in a future labour market is reflected in the way that schools are organized hierarchically with leaders at all levels taking decisions on behalf of students, though often in what is claimed to be 'their best interests', with little consultation with them or their parents despite recent legislation in England that requires all schools to have student councils.

Underpinning most decision-making in schools are deep concerns with educational and social values. An important element in this has been the concern of successive governments in England and Wales to ensure that students' moral education is clearly established and the cultures that are constructed in schools emphasize orderly activity and respect for people appointed to positions of authority by responsible bodies, such as school governors. For this reason great emphasis has been placed on keeping school assemblies, when headteachers or their delegates can emphasize the social hierarchy within which students are working, and the teaching of religious instruction, albeit from the perspective of one particular faith even though many schools now serve multi-faith communities. Since 2002, central government has required schools to teach citizenship, perhaps to complement the experiences of citizenship they gain from attending school. This framework of imposed values, based on particular social discourses related to social class, ethnic background and gender, challenges students' and staff's own constructed moral positions and the social values they have developed through their interactions with the communities, whether in school or out of school, of which they are members.

Schools, then, can be described as moral orders (Greenfield 1993) as well as communities tuned to socializing students into behaving in what dominant discourses in their host societies describe as socially appropriate ways, rather than merely as centres for producing and assessing academic knowledge. Habermas (1996) preferred to construe them as moral communities since debates and confrontations about authority and practice are based on different people's (students as well as staff) perceptions of values, attitudes and morality and their views of what people want to do with their lives. These communities are built round discourses (Habermas 1996) which are constructed by their members in their struggles to assert themselves and establish a construction of what they perceive as a truth which reflects their individual and shared values and views in the contexts in which they work and live. So in schools there is both one community, the school, and several (e.g. student friendship groups or year groups; staff groups based on subject areas/professional interests) in the formal and informal organization of a school, with the discourse of a school being constructed out of the interaction between these and within these. These discourses are framed by flows of power, whether from bureaucratic sources or from personal and professional sources of the actors – students and staff – in the communities. The outcomes of such debates are intimately bound up with the distribution of power and influence in schools and classrooms, as is discussed further in Chapter 3.

Table 1.1 Four possible approaches to making sense of organizations

The four main approaches	Structural, functional or formal systems (includes human resources views)	Cultural/ symbolic (ethnographic)	Poltical/ critical or post-structural	Personal (phenomeno-logical)
Focus	Technical–rational processes; organizational systems	People in groups constructing meanings for actions	Who has access to and projects power? How does it flow in and between social groups?	How do individuals view and interpret organizations and their place in it?
Key concerns	Accountability of participants and measuring effectiveness; sustaining successful hierarchies	How do members construct meanings and display them? What do these mean and how do these change?	Power used in whose interests? Asymmetrical power relationships scrutinized critically	How participants relate to others as groups and individuals
Assumptions	Hierarchy is necessary; maintaining organizational boundaries is important	People construct their moral orders/ communities to show values, language, rituals, symbols	Conflict can be creative; people struggle to assert their agenda against existing social systems	Individual will but also construction of self-identity is central

There are many different ways of viewing schools as institutions, as shown in Table 1.1. These complement each other by focusing on different facets of people's interactions with them. Different writers have used various terms to create such typologies.

A critical view of conventional approaches for understanding education organizations

A commonplace standpoint for understanding the management processes of educational organizations is from a rationalist or systems perspective that takes for granted the importance of making systems work. Even the more flexible variants of this, such as ambiguity theory and contingency theory, only go so far as to acknowledge that leaders and managers have to be responsive to shifting environmental contexts and therefore cannot follow preconceived plans for practice without awareness of those contexts. Ambiguity theory allows slightly greater flexibility by recognizing that leaders and managers will have to negotiate the achievement of the outcomes they desire rather than merely commanding it. So Burns (1978) has argued in favour of leaders using various types of negotiation, some of which rely on an exchange of personal wants and services (transactional leadership) and some of which rely on the creation of shared values (transformational leadership). More recent work on leadership by Hallinger and Heck (1999), for example, and on distributed leadership by Gronn (2000, 2003) does not fundamentally challenge this bifurcation of types or offer an alternative perspective, such as regarding both approaches as two of a repertoire of strategies that leaders might use in particular circumstances.

In educational leadership and management literature followers, i.e. other actors in institutions who are not leaders, are often elided with other teachers, while support staff, students and parents tend to get overlooked altogether. Indeed some recent literature that focuses on the application of Quality Management to education specifically excludes students from being actors who are part of educational institutions, casting them instead as customers. Even in recent literature on school improvement (e.g. Hopkins 2001), the focus for leaders is working with other teaching staff to raise standards of learning and teaching – a rhetoric also found in school inspection reports in England – apparently overlooking the part that students of whatever age play in helping to construct a school as an organization community as well as in constructing the learning/teaching process.

Excluding students, parents and support staff as people with agency who play a part in the construction of a school's (or college's) organizational system and social processes seems to overlook their personhood as people and it also ignores the micro-political nature of school processes that are discussed by Ball (1987), Reay (1998) and Benjamin (2002) among others and the negotiative policy processes of leadership in educational institutions analysed by Grace (1995). However, the importance of students as internal actors in the construction of a school and of schooling (Day *et al*. 2000; Flutter and Rudduck 2004), and recent central government policy in England and Wales encouraging the development of school councils where students can make their voices heard on school policy matters, point to a re-emerging awareness of the importance of encouraging students to take a responsible part in the government of their school. Parallel with this development, work by Vincent (2003) among others has underscored the importance of teachers working in partnership with parents to help develop the successful education of students, while work by Begley (1999b) and Riley *et al*. (2000) has indicated the centrality of values to the developing work of school leaders at whatever level (from class teacher through middle leader to senior management and governors) and the need for schooling to be inclusive for all students.

Commonplace discourses on leading and managing schools and colleges make assumptions that leaders always take decisions that are in the best interests of the majority of the people for whom they are responsible and that those 'best interests' fit comfortably with sustaining the current system operating in an institution, i.e. maintaining its current social processes, its current distribution of power, and its existing culture and sub-cultures in which certain norms, values and identities are privileged over others. This cosy view that sustaining existing systems comfortably meets everybody's views has to be challenged as does the assumption that leaders views reflect the norms and values of the dominant macro-culture in which a school is located. Schools are expected to reflect these as a result of various social and political pressures. So the leaders of schools are assumed to be the directors of operations who will do what is necessary to meet the greatest good of the greatest number, implementing an implicit Benthamite utilitarianism that encompasses the further marginalization of those students who have particular social or learning needs and require additional support if they are to construct a positive engagement with their school.

What systems understandings and related diagrams of organizations cannot show are the following:

- informal interactions between staff, staff and students, staff and parents
- when people 'leap-frog' lines of accountability
- participants' and external stakeholders' social and educational values and attitudes
- culture of the educational institution

- informal links with external agencies
- the effectiveness of post holders
- informal status of participants (status is only shown by title/label)
- historic aspects of relationships
- out-of-school/social networks of staff and students
- the size, condition and location of buildings and rooms
- varying workloads for different roles with the same formal label and organizational status
- the philosophy or the micro-politics of the institution.

Alternative critical perspectives

There are several different approaches to making sense of schools as organizations, as Table 1.1 showed.

This section focuses on the political model. It makes no attempt to distinguish between critical and post-structural perspectives as both focus on the use and distribution of power in institutions and societies and how this is used. A critical perspective focuses on the nexus of people's values and use power and how power flows in and around institutions and between people, institutions and their environments or contexts through micro-political and micro-cultural processes. It notes that organizations have hierarchies of power which reify the asymmetrical relationships between people that are imposed on them and explores how these hierarchies and social systems work and whose purposes they fulfil. Power is more accessible to people in more senior posts in a school hierarchy, although everybody, particularly when working in association with other participants, is able to exercise some influence in pursuit of what they would consider their legitimate goals (Hoyle 1981). People – teachers, students, senior staff, support staff – use their access to power to try to enact their agenda of educational and social values and interests, often in collaboration with other people, and position themselves in relation to other people, carrying out what Benjamin (2002) describes as micro-cultural work in the school community and its constituent sub-communities – e.g. academic and pastoral departments, year groups of students, activity interest groups, classes – as well as the broader community in which they live outside school. So people, staff as well as students, are constructing multiple identities to reflect and contribute to the variety of communities and sub-communities of which they have membership.

Political models focus on the dynamic rather than the structural aspects of organizational life, arguing that the dynamic elements shown below help to construct the structures as well as drive the changes that occur in organizations and communities.

- People have different values and attitudes – only partly shared with their colleagues.
- People in organizations have different interests in it, depending on their role, functions, beliefs, needs and perceptions, and on their social and personal lives outside school.
- People and schools are embedded in socio-political contexts which shape their processes.
- People can and do use different strategies to achieve their ends depending on their access to authority and the sources of power on which they can draw.
- Micro-political processes describe all the interactions of people in organizations, not just the vertical interactions of management theory, and take account of the differences in people's status and power.

(Hoyle 1982; Ball 1989; Foucault 1977)

Figure 1.1 shows how these different elements interact.

Figure 1.1 A different organizational model of a school

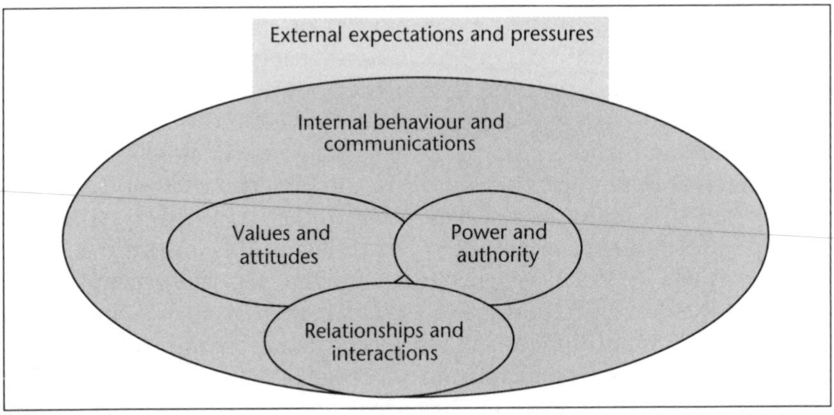

(source: Day *et al.*1990)

The interlocking and interacting of internal institutional processes with their external socio-political contexts shown in Figure 1.1 is a key element in critical and cultural understandings of the relationship of members of an organization to the organization in which they work. The internal policies and cultures of schools, reflecting socio-political pressures from national and local communities, which are mainly constructed by senior staff using varying degrees and types of consultation, serve as policy contexts for middle leaders and their colleagues in academic and pastoral departments (Busher and Barker 2003). An implication of this is that leadership in schools takes place at multiple levels (West *et al.* 2000) and is sometimes described as distributed leadership (Gronn 2000). This includes the leadership that teachers offer in the classroom (Bourdieu and Passeron 1977) through the ways in which they manage students and their learning. The histories of institutions also enshrine values which influence how leaders at all levels in a school can work. Stout *et al.* (1994: 7) discuss how these histories affected the values enshrined in schools in the New England states of the USA and how these values changed through time.

An important implication of this, as Beare *et al.* (1989) points out (see Figure 1.2), is that each school is unique and so the processes for developing it to make as successful as possible the quality of learning and teaching in it has also to be unique. One model of school improvement cannot fit all schools, although schools can certainly learn from each other's practices (Watling *et al.* 2003).

Figure 1.2 Explaining the uniqueness of each school

Anthropologically each school has unique:
- history
- socio-economic background
- traditions
- population mix
- nature and extent of cultural support and interactions with immediate and extended community
- outward and visible expressions of its culture through activities within and with its local community
- extra-curricular as well as extra-mural activities
- specialisms in its curriculum related to local community needs.

(source: Beare *et al.* 1989)

The critical perspective leaves open the possibility of wondering in whose interests head teachers (principals) and senior staff manage their schools – and middle leaders manage academic, pastoral and administrative departments – and whether the values they try to project when doing so reflect the values and needs of all students (and staff and parents, too) or whether they marginalize the actions and attitudes of some in order to promote those of others that fit more closely with the preferred values and norms of the head teacher, perhaps as he/she mediates what they claim are the preferences embedded in central and local government education policy and the views and values of local communities, as is discussed more fully in Chapter 2.

It also leaves open to question interpretations of students' behaviours and attitudes in school. Students' values and attitudes take account of the various communities inside and outside the school of which they have membership and the conflicting demands these might make of them. It considers the distribution of power in a school and the manifestation of that in school decision-making systems to be problematic, rather than taken for granted, and so raises questions about why a school is structured in a certain way, why students are allocated to particular classes or why resources are allocated in particular ways. So it can debate what constitutes social justice and equity in school policy when a school serves a wide diversity of communities and individual students' needs and why some student behaviours are constructed as misbehaviours while others are not (Foucault 1977). It questions how those behaviours are interpreted in the different communities inside and outside the school to which a student belongs and why some interpretations of behaviour rather than others are privileged in the school community. It raises questions about why some types of students are excluded more frequently from schools than others, how the student and her/his parents or carers understand the administrative processes for managing those (mis)behaviours, and the extent to which they feel able to exert influence within the administrative system that manages them so that they emerge with a sense of justice and dignity. Built into this is a notion of administrative justice (Riddell 2003): so long as the processes of decision-making are operated fairly, as perceived by all parties involved, then whatever decision is reached can be construed as a reasonable decision. It led Bacharach (1983) to argue that:

- education organizations are best conceived as political systems;
- participants conceived as political actors with their own needs/ values, objectives, strategies;
- decision-making is the primary arena of political conflict.

(in Westoby 1988: 282)

Figure 1.3 tries to capture this perspective on decision-making processes in schools.

This book sets out to explore the implications of a critical perspective for understanding the processes of leadership at senior, middle and classroom level. By implication this also has to take account of the voices of students and their parents and carers as they, too, are part of a school community and share in its construction even if it is led by teaching staff. The discussion of leadership is presented through a series of chapters drawing in many cases on research evidence from a variety of sources. It begins by discussing the interrelationship of schools with their socio-political and economic contexts, as well as debating how these interact with and penetrate the semi-permeable membrane of the school organizational boundary, before moving on to discuss one of the central themes of this perspective, the construction of power and the processes of using it through micro-political processes. As part of this discussion, how knowledge is shaped by distributions of power at institutional and classroom level is discussed. However, as education is a value-laden activity and values are central to much education decision-making, the importance of values and culture to the construction of schooling are discussed not only because of their intrinsic importance but also because they are foci of power for individuals and groups or collectivities (Lukes 1974). Since values are important and one of the key questions in a critical perspective is how is power used and in whose interests, a theme of social justice and inclusion runs through the discussions in the book since it addresses concerns about how those with less social capital may be helped to benefit as much from education as those who have more, at least, to start with in life.

Figure 1.3 Leading in education: learning, teaching, leading in community
           contexts

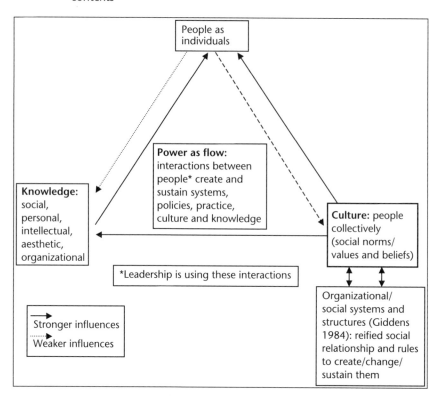

2 Mediating the external policy contexts of schools

Mediating and mapping the contexts

Leaders are mediators of the social and curriculum contexts of schools for staff, students and parents (Busher and Barker 2003) to make teaching and learning relevant and appropriately differentiated, as Krechevsky and Stork (2000) found, as well as compliant with internal and external policy-makers' demands and values. Making choices about values and actions involves leaders and their colleagues in moral decisions about the nature of the learning community they want to construct. It means that values are central to the field of educational administration (Willower 1992). Ribbins (1999) remarked that privileging some values over others is a political act – applying power to sustain some actions in preference to others. Moos (2000) points out the impact on schooling and education of globalization; of the OECD emphasizing decentralized finances in the 1980s; and of models of New Public Management (NPM) emphasizing systems thinking, personal mastery and tight hands-on management, explicit standards and measures of performance. Woods (1996: 15) complained that a narrow and 'distorted view of consumerism, that can only be found in the unreal world of the perfect market, has dominated the rhetoric and shaped the educational debates' of the last two decades of the twentieth century in the UK. Kazmi (1998: 86) points out that there are similar problems and tensions in India between 'the demands of materialistic values imitated from western societies' and his own cultural heritage. In Saudi Arabia, this macro-cultural framework for education is made explicit. There the purposes of education were said to be

> basically reflected in the maintenance of its faith, security and stability, besides achieving the development according to the broad concept as well as its economic and social dimension. Consequently the objectives of higher education in the Kingdom have been designed in a way to interpret this concept ... as follows:

- Develop the belief of loyalty to God besides providing students with Islamic culture that makes them sense their responsibility towards God so that their practical and scientific potentials would be perfectly useful and fruitful. The Kingdom alone has been strictly adhering to this goal

- Preparing citizens to be scientifically and intellectually qualified so as to shoulder their responsibilities towards their country and nation according to sound principles of the Islamic faith

- Enable the citizens to play a positive role in the field of scientific research which contributes to the development of the society in all walks of life

- Avail an opportunity to talented students to join postgraduate programs in various scientific specializations

- Activate literary and scientific work in the service of Islamic thought so as to enable the country to shoulder its role in contributing to civilization by adhering to genuine Islamic principles aimed at averting materialistic and heretical deviation

- Translate useful arts and sciences into Arabic, the language of the Holy Qur'an, besides developing scientific Arabic vocabulary to substitute the foreign technical terms

- Provide training services to the graduates so as to acquaint them with the latest development in areas of their specializations.

(Kamel 1998)

These macro-policy contexts are also active at local or regional level (Riley *et al.* 2000; Busher and Barker 2003), sometimes called the mesosphere, and include the impact on the curriculum and on staff, student and parent relationships of schools' civic communities and communities where people live as well as local or regional government.

The above extract also indicates the influence of another context that shapes education, that of faith. At about the same date in Britain Sir Ron Dearing was reviewing the practices of schools run by the Church of England to help them try to ensure that their work was underpinned clearly by a specifically Christian ethic (*Guardian*, 7 January 2000). So the definition of the purposes of education depends on the hegemonic discourses in

a society and who are the powerful people able to influence the establishment of core values for education in particular social contexts (*TES*, 21
January 2005). For example, Tim Brighouse argues for a system of schooling
that balances the needs of individuals with the need to strengthen communities (*TES*, 21 January 2005) but other influential people or bodies
might argue for a system of schooling that helps young people prepare for
a life of servitude in offices and factories – although such arguments are
usually couched in terms of preparing them vocationally to hold a job successfully.

It is usually powerful people and groups in a society who are more
influential in asserting their views to construct an agenda for education.
Foucault (1976) points out how knowledge is constructed through the operation of power, and what comes to be accepted in society as truth, or in this
case, as appropriate education and processes of schooling, depends on the
interplay of various political factors and factions that struggle to assert their
view of how things should be.

In England and Wales this is evident in the wave of reforms in education put in place by central government legislation between 1986 and 1993,
sweeping away the power of teachers over the curriculum and of local
authorities over the schools in their geo-political areas. Both collectivities
have been largely replaced by a strongly centrally directed system of education. At the same time a charade of public choice was created (Edwards *et
al.* 1989) and a veneer of site-based management of school operations put
in place by devolving budgetary responsibility to each school from the LAs
(local authorities) in which they were located. The flexibility that schools
have in which to manage their budgets is very limited as essential staffing,
equipment and consumables swallow most of their income. In 1993 the
new system of site-based school management was sealed in place with the
inception of a piece of bureaucratic surveillance: the creation of the Office
for Standards in Education (OFSTED) which was responsible for inspecting
all schools in England and Wales. Foucault (1977) pointed out the importance of surveillance as a means whereby systems assert their power over
individual people, and powerful people in systems assert their influence
over less powerful people. OFSTED, a quango of central government,
inspects schools and the teachers in them in England and Wales every four
years to make sure they conform to rigorous standards of performance laid
out in the OFSTED criteria for evaluating schools. It retains this responsibility even when schools carry out their own self-evaluation. Schools that
do not meet these standards are punished or, if they fail badly, are closed.
In both cases the punishment falls on the staff who work in these schools
since it is teachers who are sacked or forced to resign from their jobs, and
on the students who are demoralized to discover that powerful authorita-
tive voices (the inspectors) thought they were working in poor schools
(Busher and Barker 2003). Only in the early twenty-first century were

schools again encouraged to evaluate their own practice, albeit within OFSTED guidelines and monitoring.

Surveillance of schools was also developed by central government through publishing annual national league tables of schools' students' performances in public examinations. These were said to help parents make choices about which schools to choose for their children but they also gave OFSTED important information about how schools were performing compared with each other. The league tables took no account, until 2004, of the different social communities that different schools served, how that affected the performance of the students in them or the value (incremental gains) which teachers and schools added to student achievement. Further, it helped to strengthen state and institutional surveillance over students by shifting the emphasis in education from helping students individually to develop intellectually, emotionally and socially, to focusing on their performances as members of and producers for their schools as corporations. Product here refers to the knowledge constructed by students, specifically that academic knowledge assessed by public examinations. It is tempting to see this as a late twentieth-century conduit for reintroducing the factory system into education in England and Wales, equivalent to the monitorial system of teaching used in the mid-nineteenth century.

Driving this development of the education system was a neo-liberal ideology put forward by people such as Hayek (Gamble 1996) which assumed that the marketplace was the best means of distributing social goods such as education. This completely overlooked the impact of people's social capital (Bourdieu 1990) which shaped their ability to access education and limited parents' choices about what sorts of education to access for their children. The impact of having limited social capital is seen most clearly in the work of Thrupp (1999) and Wells (1996) who point out the impact of socio-economic status on children's and parents' choices of schooling in New Zealand and the USA and on their subsequent success at school.

If these contexts of education and schooling are so important and influential on the internal institutional processes of schools, then a crucial question is how their influence is conveyed to those internal processes in such a way as to affect the organizational cultures of schools as well as their legal bureaucratic structures. The rest of this chapter explores how external factors influence and are influenced by the internal policy and decision-making processes of a school.

External and internal policy processes

The current contexts of a school can be divided up into its external national and local policy contexts and its internal policy processes. There are also external social and economic contexts nationally and locally. The external policy contexts relevant to a study in England include central and local government policies as well as shifts in public attitudes and the socio-economic status of members of the communities that each school serves (Riley *et al.* 2000; Busher and Barker 2003). The contexts from central government in England include policies such as the National Curriculum, Key Stage 3 strategies and the introduction of performance management, as well as those that have already been discussed. These are complemented by curriculum frameworks policed by public examination boards on behalf of central government. At local or regional government level are policies defining from which communities a school's students may come, what levels of support particular students might receive, and how students said to have behavioural difficulties can be helped.

How policy is developed in central and local arenas of government is summarized by Figure 2.1 (see page 17). It shows the incoherence of policy inception and the non-linearity of policy development, shaped by the ebb and flow of power wielded by influential pressure groups and erratic critical incidents in national and local life. For example, in the 1960s and 1970s national attention was focused by a series of incidents on the need for a national framework for the school curriculum (Ball and Bowe 1992). In the early twenty-first century the Victoria Climbié report focused government policy on uniting the provision of child support services, including schools, to avoid another child dying because her mistreatment at home was not noticed sufficiently quickly by relevant local authority services. It led to the White Paper 'Every child matters' (2002) and the Children's Act (2004) which have radically altered the framework within which education is managed in England. Rational models of policy development try to disguise these critical processes behind tidy functional processes that are said to show national, local and institutional life but prevent exploration of the asymmetrical power relationships that exist in these bureaucracies at all levels and the shifts in balances and flows of power which disturb them from time to time and bring about change.

The internal policies of institutions, and their affiliated cultures, are constructed, negotiated and projected by a school's senior management team (Grace 1995). The internal policies of schools that are constructed by senior management serve as policy contexts for middle leaders and their colleagues in academic and pastoral departments (Busher and Barker 2003). An implication of this is that leadership in schools takes place at multiple levels (West *et al.* 2000) and is sometimes described as distributed leadership (Gronn 2000). The histories of institutions also act as a context, enshrining values that influence how leaders at all levels in that organization can work. Stout *et al.* (1994: 7) discuss how these histories affected the values enshrined in schools in the New England states of the USA and how these values changed through time.

Figure 2.1 A model for analysing policy implementation

Drivers of policy
Ideology
Economy, e.g. globalization
Strategic positioning of (government or institution)
Preferred social structures

Development of policy
(policy trajectory: from idea [inception] → agenda → planning → implementation → coordination); policy borrowing from other countries/societies

Inception – in the light of policy drivers and perceived threats; key people (policy conceivers, policy shapers, policy amplifiers, policy selectors – see also communications nodes); pressure groups; interest groups; bureaucracies; politicians

Centres of power and influences – think tanks; quangos; local and national government offices; bureaucracies; arenas of discussion (research; scenario building – also used for strategic development); communications nodes; all make use of: communications (including ICT) networks; formal and informal (grapevine); press (briefings and stories, leaks) and media

Agenda – acceptance and promulgation of policy; consultation on policy development (scenario building; Green Papers/White Papers); gathering allies; control of information

Planning, implementation and coordination – legislation; national programmes; administrative memoranda and circulars; national and local launches; key people (policy implementers) gathering allies; selecting personnel to spearhead

---

As members of the school community, like any other actors in it, students help intentionally or unintentionally to construct its culture and the teaching and learning processes in which they engage and in which they are guided and managed by their teachers. The term 'student' is preferred here and throughout the book to that of 'pupil' since the former is the term more commonly used internationally for children and young people who attend a school or college.

Students cannot be outcomes or products of a school as they are sentient people, not objects, although, like any other member of it, they will be shaped by their experiences in it and of it, and will help to shape or influence its processes to a greater or lesser extent. Giddens (1979) emphasizes the difference between things and people, the latter always having agency through which they struggle to interact with other people and the social and organizational systems and structures around them. Like other communities, schools have webs of interconnectedness above and beyond the contractual relationships that may initially define people's membership of them (Sergiovanni 1994). It is through these rather than through formal structures that students influence the development of school cultures and communities. However, recent central government initiatives (2002) to promote school councils as part of the agenda of student inclusion have given national policy legitimation to efforts to include students formally in school decision-making – belated recognition of the evidence from various educators, such as Rudduck *et al.* (1996) or Cooper and McIntyre (1996), let alone that of radical approaches to schooling, that students of all ages develop reasoned and reasonable views of more and less effective school practices and can play a sensible part in school decision-making.

Other people in the local civic communities around schools, such as parents and education officers, who are in conventional senses outside the organizational boundaries of a school (although Gray (1991) debates this), also shape the internal management and curriculum processes of schooling (Busher 1989, 2002) informally if not formally, as do parent and community governors on school governing bodies. In each case, of course, they pursue their own or their communities' interests in constructing their agenda for how schools should develop. It raises questions about which groups of people are able to assert what influence in whose interests and how they construct and project that influence. The range of these constituencies or stakeholder groups are shown in Figure 2.2 but the boundaries are to some extent arbitrary.

Figure 2.2 External and internal constituencies of a school

External
- past and future students
- local social and community groups
- local government officers and policy-makers
- central government representatives and policy-makers
- local employers
- past and future parents
- past teachers

Internal
- current students
- teaching staff
- support staff
- present parents
- school governors

(source: Busher 1998)

Social contexts and the semi-permeable membranes of school boundaries

How the internal processes of schools are influenced by their external environments has been poorly researched (Glatter 1997). Systems models of organizations claim that it is senior staff in an institution who police its boundaries, filtering down or mediating to other staff in an establishment the external policies and pressure confronting it. This overlooks the social realities that all members of an institution are in touch with some aspects of the external environment of an institution even though senior staff may be the only ones in contact with crucial information about it such as finances or the legal framework or, in the case of educational institutions, recruitment of students. In this, schools are like other service industries.

Teachers' contacts with the civic community occur intentionally as part of their job, through formal events such as parents' consultations, or school events to which parents and other members of the local community are invited, or through direct liaison with individual parents of individual students. They also occur unintentionally, for example, when the outcomes of dual-use facilities impinge on teachers' practices. For example, the use of one school at weekends for community classes left teachers with a considerable amount of litter and chaos to clear up on a Monday morning, so several claimed, before they could begin to teach (Busher 1992).

At another level the interactions of schools and their civic communities is an informal process embodied in the personnel working in schools. Students, teachers and support staff living in the communities a school serves bring with them into school the views about the school held in those communities. The views about the school which students and staff express in their everyday contacts in their communities affect the way in which the school is perceived (Busher and Saran 2000). Such views are likely to reflect on how effectively a school is managed as well as reflecting the values and attitudes of those students and staff living in those communities. In some cases communities' views will affect how a school organizes particular activities, such as the lunchtime break (Busher 1989), as is illustrated in Vignette 2.1.

These contacts with civic communities shape the interactions of teachers and students in the arena of the classroom, affecting teachers' interests in curriculum and pedagogic matters, as is shown in Vignette 2.1. The attitudes of students' parents also affect the relationships between teachers and pupils in a school, and affect the ways in which teachers are able to wield their authority. One subject leader commented how he frequently had to talk with his students about tolerance because of the bigoted views they brought from home into school (Busher 2002). This links closely with the work of Thrupp (1999), Wells (1996) and Lauder and Hughes (1999) who suggest that students' home influences have a much greater impact on the outcomes of their schooling than does the effective management of schools, a view sustained by Creemers (1994), one of the leading lights in School Effectiveness research, and also by Mortimore and Whitty (1997).

Vignette 2.1 Influences of communities on schools

June's sense of answerability had several dimensions ... one of which was generated by the geo-social parameters of the catchment area of the school ... several administrative procedures that constrained her work as a teacher arose out of the nature of the catchment area ... many pupils were bussed into school ... making it difficult for her to keep pupils in detention after school ... The school's rolling lunch system made it difficult for her to monitor individual pupils' social and academic performance, as pupils whom she wanted to see could be dining at a different time from herself.

The answerability of teachers to the community was often mediated by senior staff. For example the implementation of the rolling lunch system was because senior staff feared the school might get a reputation for ill-disciplined pupils at lunchtime ... the first and second year pupils had been taught on a separate school site, but when the sites were amalgamated under pressure from the LEA [sic], senior staff were appalled at the number of pupils milling around at lunchtime... senior staff were also concerned with pupils' academic performance, as was June, in part to attract the more able pupils from local primary schools against the competition from other local secondary schools.

The socio-cultural perspectives of the local community, especially as mediated to her by senior staff, also affected June's work. The senior staff believed that the community wanted ... the school to be well-ordered ... As one deputy head put it, 'We run a tight ship here.' This conflicted with June's philosophy of teaching which focused on helping pupils to learn by whatever means they could understand, and helping people to feel valued. One consequence of senior staff emphasis on order was that June had to uphold school dress codes for pupils ... leading her sometimes into a more authoritarian relationship with pupils than she liked. A second consequence was that senior staff tried to regulate the dress of teachers. June recounted how she and another young female teacher had been asked by the headteacher not to wear trousers to school.

(source: Busher 1989)

Student influences on school organizational processes

As might be expected, students, too, bring into school values and views held in their communities which are often expressed through their actions in corridors and playgrounds as well as through comments in class (Busher 1992). These values and attitudes have considerable influence on the strategies teachers may use to manage classrooms and sustain effective discipline in a school. O'Connor (1997) pointed out how students' views were affected by their gender and ethnicity. How teachers respond to students and manage situations with them depends in part on how teachers interpret students' behaviours and needs, and on how teachers respond personally to the situation in which they find themselves. Teachers are often acutely aware of pupils' interactions and how these influence the way they manage lessons, as is shown in Vignette 2.2.

Vignette 2.2 Pupils as co-creators and mediators of school cultures

'It depends on what I expect of particular pupils ... on my mood ... it might be that the headmaster is teaching next door ... I don't like him to see them getting very disruptive, not that the kids care ... [but] it's expected that I make them work.'

... June was acutely aware of the pupils' interactions and said this influenced how she managed her lessons. At one level she said she was concerned that some pupils ... could and would subvert her agenda ... so she did not like to see pupils sitting around not working during lessons ... She objected to pupils coming in late to her lessons and then asking other pupils to get out of what they saw as 'their' seats. She insisted that late pupils sat where she put them.

... June's knowledge of pupils' social networks allowed her to make fine adjustments to the management of her lessons ... stopping certain pupils sitting together to minimise disruption ... knowledge of individual pupils allowed her to differentiate her reactions to the same behaviour by different pupils ... 'If Paul turns round talking, I know he hasn't got it [notes] down. But if James did, then I would know that he had got it down.'

Pupils also influenced June's actions through her understanding of what it meant to be a teacher, her concern for the welfare of her pupils. In academic work ... this took the form of allowing pupils to use whatever mathematical methodology worked for them in solving problems ... 'With my remedial class [sic] I use less formal teaching. I've got five [in the group] and we work all the time on the blackboard or in little groups.'

(source: Busher 1989)

In more extreme cases the values and behaviour that students bring in to school from the external environment can affect teachers' conceptions of themselves as individuals. 'The stress that half a dozen kids, even in a school like this, can create among teachers is just out of proportion to the rest of the things that go on' (Busher 1992: 190). Teachers in the same study noted how relationships with difficult students affected their relationships with other more cooperative students and with their colleagues on the staff. Not least, the inability to control students successfully was seen as a weakness in staff who consequently lost esteem in the views of their colleagues. In the case of subject leaders and middle managers, the ability to control students was perceived by colleagues as a source of esteem and, in effect, a source of expert power (Busher 2002). Rudduck *et al.* (1996) also noted the influence that students had on teachers' performances and the perceptiveness that they had of the quality of teachers' performances.

The impact of national and local policy contexts on the internal processes of schools

Schools are situated in socio-political contexts, as is shown in Figure 2.3, which affect the ways in which teachers in schools can act. In some cases their choice of action is limited by the outcome of national and local policy decisions, as in the case of the assisted places scheme (Edwards *et al.* 1989), as well as by the competence of their local education authorities (Busher and Barker 2003) in England and Wales.

Figure 2.3 External contexts of schooling

- of values
- of policy at national level
- of local government
- of resources
- of markets (quality assurance and client choice)
- of technology (what may or can be created or produced)
- of civic communities
- of pedagogical knowledge
- of management knowledge

(source: Busher 1998)

The literature on school effectiveness provides an important description of the national policy framework in England and its impact on schools. Both Sammons and Mortimore (1997) and the most recent (2002) OFSTED handbook for secondary schools give clear indications of the characteristics that schools and their departments need to construct to be considered effective. Schools that fail to recognize the power of this external socially constructed definition of successful schooling and perform inadequately compared with it are considered to be failing and can be closed.

In order to retain public confidence, school leaders need to be aware of the demands being made of them by the external environment. It is not just senior staff who have to be aware of the impact of these policy contexts on schools, as systems models of organizations would have readers believe, but staff at all levels in an organization, and students too. Teachers and support staff who were interviewed in two separate research projects by Busher and Blease (2000) and Busher and Saran (2000) gave clear evidence of this awareness, as is shown in Figure 2.4.

Individual teachers' awareness of national or local government initiatives in some cases led them to offer to manage particular curriculum processes. Busher (1992: 182) reported how one teacher responded to one of the then national priorities for funded in-service education. 'The last thing I noticed came up was something about AIDS. You know there's been a directive come down to schools about it: you've got to teach kids about AIDS.' As a science teacher she was interested in helping promote students,'! health education, but only held a minor promoted post. The senior staff of the school needed somebody to manage this curriculum development for the whole school, but had nobody to do so, until this science teacher volunteered. Her explanation was that taking on this work matched her curriculum interests and developed her managerial expertise.

Local authority policies also affect the creation and implementation of policy in schools in England and Wales. The importance of these local policy contexts is illustrated by the example of a school in special measures which was required by its OFSTED inspection report to improve the quality of its management as well as to improve the quality of teaching and learning. At the same time as making these changes, successive head teachers of the school had to negotiate with the LA to ensure that the school remained open (Busher and Barker 2003) as the local authority was reorganizing secondary schooling in its area. These negotiations were not cold-eyed boundary management by the head teachers but the cut and thrust of pressure group politics. Internal school management and educational processes developed in a symbiotic relationship with external political processes: Demonstrable improvements in the school's management and quality of teaching and learning were of political importance in countering local authority plans to close it as well as of educational importance in improving the quality of education. The diminution of the threat of closure by the local authority, also helped the school to climb out of special measures, not least by helping to restore morale to staff and students.

Figure 2.4 Staff awareness of national policy contexts and school processes

Financial pressures in the external environment of schools affect their internal processes:

- *LMS has brought greater emphasis on value for money* (Science Technician)
- *trying to repair things rather than replace ... [the] budget is too low for necessary repainting of classrooms. This might depress the morale of staff and pupils* (Premises Officer)

This in turn affected the way in which staff as individuals perceived their jobs. It affected their morale: *because people are having to work much harder with no increase in pay. Since overtime has been cut people are reluctant to use their own time to do extra jobs* (Premises Officer)

It also had an effect on how a school could be managed: *there has been a decline in the quality of work because of a 50 per cent decline in hours [available for work]* (Premises Officer); *cleaning is being done as cheaply as possible so there has been a decline in quality* (Teacher)

It affected the quality of learning and teaching: *Poor quality environment will affect the pupils* (Teacher; Premises Officer) because students would take less care of and have less enthusiasm for their work if the physical environment is poorly maintained and there is not sufficient equipment available for them to undertake interactive work, such as laboratory work in the sciences

There were concerns about job security, too, because of extensive restructuring of ancillary staff work and budgetary pressures on teachers' posts. Only amongst clerical staff was there an increase in employment opportunities in part because schools individually could not achieve the same economies of scale in employing staff as could LEAs [*sic*]:

- *We've got a registrar who does for us what used to be done by County Hall* (Technician)
- *There is now so much more paperwork for care taking and maintenance* (Bursar)
- *Using LMS to save costs has led to a reduction in staffing* (Science Technician)
- *Can't get technical support for the department* (Head of Department)
- *Will have to cut caretaking staff and we have got rid of most of our midday supervisors ... replacing them with volunteer teachers and reducing the length of lunchtime* (Head of Department)

(source: Busher and Saran 2000)

Individual teachers, as well as senior staff, are aware of how links with their schools' local authorities are important for developing aspects of their and their students' work. Some teachers in the past have used LA advisers to gain support for curriculum developments, allowing them to implement curriculum change or negotiate additional resources from their head teachers (Busher 1992). Other teachers have found LA support valuable for programmes of curriculum and staff development (Harris 2000), while yet others recognized the importance of inter-school collaboration (Busher and

Hodgkinson 1996) to staff development whether promoted by LAs or developed by schools on their own. The success of the Nottingham IQEA project (Watling *et al.* 2003) depended on successful inter-school collaboration. In many schools senior staff perceive the development of strong contacts with other schools in their family or cluster as an important means of helping student transition (Galton *et al.* 1999) and head teachers of secondary schools perceive such links with primary schools as an important means of recruiting students at the end of Key Stage 2.

Not all pressures from external policy contexts of schools, however, are positive. When staff withdraw from activities it is often due to other or new pressures from these contexts, leaving them with insufficient time to pursue professional interests in which they are already engaged. A particular example of innovation inundation was the continual flow of organizational change demanded of schools in England in the 1990s. This led to a diminution of the amount of extra-mural activities teachers were willing to undertake, whether in the form of fieldwork or sports activities. In 1998 in some schools it also took the form of members of some teachers' unions refusing to engage in more than one organizational meeting a week. They argued that proliferation of such activities were not part of their core work as circumscribed by the allocation of directed time (Teachers' Pay and Conditions Act, 1987).

Foucault (1975) discusses how institutions are both sites for the enactment of power and conduits through which power from other sources can be passed. So, for example, students are controlled by teachers in schools not only representing their own authority as leaders of developing learning and constructing the curriculum in the institution but also as, in some way, agents of government policies. The conduits by which schools, teachers and students receive messages from the external policy contexts also mediate the messages that they hear. In some cases these mediating agencies and agents seriously distort the messages. The extent and complexity of these conduits is shown in Table 2.1. Not all external agencies to schools are equally powerful since some hold more direct power (involvement through statute law; control of resources) over schools than others. Further, schools are able to influence the processes of many of those external agencies that are in a school's local community through political action, so long as there are appropriate individual people to engage in that action. Indeed many head teachers seek to engage in such action through negotiations with their schools' local authorities. A key source of power to sustain head teachers in their discussions with local authorities is the effectiveness with which their school is running (Busher and Barker 2003). Thus practices and changes in the internal workings of a school are both influenced by and themselves can be used to influence processes in the external environment of schools.

Table 2.1 Mediating contexts of schooling to school staff and students

Contexts	Mediators: agencies	Mediators: agents	Interpreters of contexts	Factors shaping people's interpretations
Cultural, social and educational values	Government papers, e.g. DfES circulars	LA education officers	Senior staff	Personal and professional interests[1]
Policy at national level	Newspapers and national media	School governors	Middle leaders, e.g. curriculum coordinators	Formal role(s) in school
Policy at local government	Local newspapers and media	Senior staff	Teachers	Informal role(s) in school
Resource	Professional papers, e.g. TES	Parents	Learning support staff	Networks and contacts in and out of school
Markets (client choice)	OFSTED (inspectors)	Support staff	Secretarial staff	Educational and social values
Technology (what can be produced)	Local authority	Teaching staff	Site staff	Gender
Civic communities		Students	Students	Social class
Knowledge: teaching, learning, management		Community leaders	Parents	Ethnic background[2]

Notes: [1] Busher (2001). [2] O'Connor (1997).

What a model of schools in their environments might look like

The foregoing argument develops a view of how the external contexts of a school penetrate all its processes not only through a hierarchically filtered model but through direct intervention at every level of a school. Figure 2.5 is an attempt at a linear and static representation of what is, perforce, a dynamic three-dimensional model of time, space and people. In this model, each group of actors brings views and values from the external environment into the internal processes of schools. Weber and Mitchell (1999) point out the important influence of the media on teachers' opinions as well as on other people's view of teachers' actions.

Figure 2.5 Conduits of power

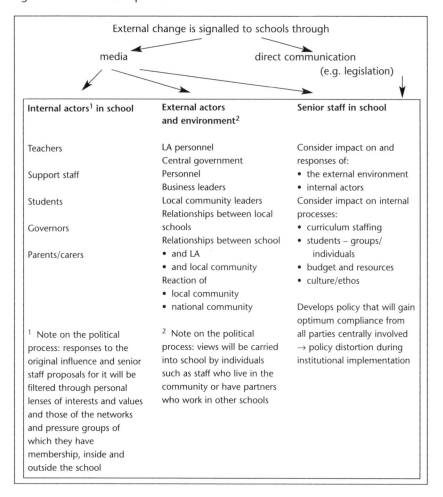

These external influences and the conduits through which they are channelled affect the management processes of schools and their departments both in posing problems to which staff have to respond and in shaping the range of decisions that individual staff are willing or able to take. Staff, particularly the more senior staff, are also concerned to ensure that people in school meet organizational goals that are often prescribed by external agencies of national government. The school thus becomes an arena in which personal, professional and organizational interests are negotiated to meet the competing and consensual agenda of a large number of people in them as well as those of people and policy-makers in their external contexts. However, not all people in this model have equal power.

Emerging concepts: a putative research agenda

The interaction between external contexts and internal management processes

The situations with which teachers and school leaders at various levels have to deal is often defined in the dialogue between external stakeholders and powerbrokers and themselves. This is not cold-eyed boundary management but pressure group politics, however politely sustained. Key questions here for school leaders are: who are your allies? What are the tensions between allies? Some other internal actors in a school also have powerful external connections, making them either important assets to a school in its struggle for leverage over external pressures or serious threats if they are pursuing agenda that diverge from the aims of the school or the policies of the senior staff. Powerful external pressures at national and local level can define what actions a school may take internally.

Internal management processes on their own are an insufficient focus to understand change in schools. Appropriate management processes for change cannot be prescribed regardless of the contexts in which they have to operate, if they are to be successful. So there is also a need to take account of the views and values of a wide variety of stakeholders in a school and what they hope to gain from particular situations or fear from particular changes. There is also a need to take account of how internal processes impact on external socio-political processes.

The civic community as important stakeholder in school performance

The local community through parents and other people who use a school, e.g. religious groups who hire a school's premises, have a keen interest in the success of a school – see for example the work of Vincent (2003). In times of crisis if they are satisfied with a school they will support it (Busher

and Barker 2003). A school can build up this community support by including parents and others in school activities; by acknowledging local cultural
life through the ceremonial activities of a school; and by consulting parents
over major decisions being taken by a school. Fostering school–community
activities also helps to strengthen community support. How a civic community penetrates school life at many levels and the quality of local
community life affects the quality of life in a school and the expectations that
students and parents have of a school. Students' and parents' views of and
attitudes to a school are also likely to affect both the range of management strategies that might be appropriate or those that it is reasonable to
implement.

Students are key players in internal school processes

Students as participants in a school both build a sense of school community and develop processes of constructing learning with each other and
with their teachers; students are not just consumers or 'customers'. School
students do not play a passive role in their own education but help to construct the processes of learning as well as the social processes of schooling
but do so within the framework of the social communities they inhabit
outside school. These external communities affect their attitudes to and
behaviours in school. Teachers need to recognize the degree to which
young people shape the culture of their school and so the need to adopt
different strategies with different students to enlist them as challenging
partners in curricular and extra-curricular contexts. Linear, rationalist
models of development seem to neglect the diverse interests, needs and
aspirations that shape the response of students and their teachers.

Political understandings of processes are crucial

Political understandings of internal decision-making processes are crucial –
see for example the work of Ball (1987) and Grace (1995). Especially in a
crisis there is flux. These processes are rationalized into systems understandings but in reality are constructed from people seeking to serve their
interests, although these may be held professionally/altruistically with the
intention of meeting the needs of others, e.g. students. This is an anti-func-
tionalist perspective – people are complex beings, not cogs in a machine,
who try to balance the demands of their organizational lives against those
of their social lives and their values and beliefs.

Individuals, groups and organizations tend to adopt a range of competing and collusive strategies informed by their varied needs and perspectives. OFSTED prompted local politicians, officers, governors, head
teachers and teachers to micro-political calculation and manoeuvre rather
than educational development. For example, attempts to restructure

schools radically undermine established social structures and so challenge every participant's assumptions about themselves. Parents and community residents near a school are likely to interpret such events as an attack on the school and community.

Individual perspectives on organizational process

People in school communities act in particular ways because of a wide variety of factors, only some of which reflect the formal posts they occupy and the formal responsibilities for which they are accountable. How they will respond to changes in the external and internal policy and social contexts of their work will depend on a variety of factors. To explain their choice of action then raises questions about their beliefs, interests/aims, perspectives, knowledge and skills. People's individual histories and life experiences shape their interactions in the here and now. What point they have reached in their personal and professional life cycle (Goodson 1992) will also affect their choices: people at different stages of careers and personal lives want different goals, are able to achieve different qualities of performance; individuals at different stages of development will work more or less well together.

Influenced by long-established ideas and attitudes, teachers tend to deny or embrace the agenda that is created for them by senior staff. In circumstances of flux, while some staff create new careers in school improvement, learning the approved technique of action plans and targets, others withdraw themselves from the classroom and eventually from education.

3 Where power lies within schools

Developing a political understanding of school organizations

At the heart of everyday life in schools lies the interactions of people: teachers with students, teachers with teachers, teachers with parents, teachers with senior staff – and vice versa. A political model of organizations offers a dynamic and negotiative framework for understanding these interactions whether they are in the realm of management, the realm of ideas, values and beliefs, or the realm of people's social and interpersonal needs (Duignan and McPherson 1992). Some effort has been made to chart this model (Ball 1987), by describing the ways in which actors engage with the social systems and structures (Giddens 1979) that surround them, and the ways that leaders and teachers in schools engage with each other (Hoyle 1986) to achieve policies and practices that are claimed to meet the needs of the students, at least in the view of the dominant people in the school, or in a department of a school if the analysis focuses on such a sub-unit. An analysis of micro-political processes views educational institutions as arenas of contestations of values, which guide the implementation of practices, through political negotiations and policy processes (Grace 1995) and offers a holistic explanation for the interactions of people in organizations (Ball 1989) not merely a top-down view as managerial discourses tend to do. In these interactions participants (senior staff, teachers, support staff, students, parents) are actors with their own interests and values that they want to see implemented in practice through the accession of adequate resources to them. Gaining access to these resources requires actors to use different sources of power (French and Raven 1968; Sergiovanni 1995) in support of their preferred goals. However, these are contested, as many actors want access to the same scarce resources for different goals, leading inevitably to some members of a school resisting the implementation of policies and practices proposed by others. In a political model this is perceived as a normally occurring aspect of social and organizational life (van der Westhuisen 1996) rather than an indication of pathological malaise.

The importance of this political model to making sense of the work of teachers and students in schools emerged very clearly in a small-scale study of how some middle leaders in some secondary schools led their departments and negotiated with their colleagues and with the senior management team of their schools to implement preferred practices for teaching and learning and staff development in their subject areas, albeit within the framework of the development plans of the schools. These subject and pastoral leaders represent only partially the wide diversity of work carried out by middle leaders and of their attitudes to that work, but, none the less, form part of that realm of the middle discussed by Siskin (1994) and more recently by Bennett *et al.* (2003). It is these middle leaders, especially in larger schools, who help to create subject-related and pastoral policies, often in negotiation with their colleagues, to implement the policies of themselves, of senior management and those required by central government through the construction of particular practices in the 'classroom'. This term is used loosely here and throughout this book to refer to any organized arena in which learning is intended to take place. Through these policies middle leaders try to project power to shape decisions to promote their own preferred values and visions of successful practice.

All people in educational institutions have access to some sources of power (Hoyle 1981), including teachers, support staff, students and their parents and carers. Howard and Gill (2000) show how acutely children are aware of political processes and power in schools. Smyth *et al.* (2000) discuss how teachers' in the course of their professional development have to contend with the realities of power in schools and educational systems. A model showing where power may flow in educational organizations is shown in Figure 3.1 (see page 33). This is because, as Greenfield (1993) points out, social systems are made up of individuals. But people are not homogeneous. As each actor has a different personality or personhood (Aubrey *et al.* 2000) which has been constructed with various values, beliefs and perspectives (Giddens 1991), personality is also part of the process of social interaction and affects how participants engage with policies and policy processes.

As a consequence, more successful leaders in schools try to be emotionally literate (Goleman 1995) by recognizing the social, emotional and intellectual needs of the students and staff who work with them (Day *et al.* 2000) and of parents, too. In Western anglophone macro-cultures they seem to achieve this by creating organizational cultures based on authentic relationships (Hopkins *et al.* 1997b) between people. Successful cultures are defined by Hargreaves (1994) as collegial rather than just professionally collaborative (McGregor 2000), meaning that they are constructed between equals. But the asymmetrical formal power relationships in hierarchical organizations like schools do not allow this equality to occur, making it seem that respectful collaborative relationships are probably the best that can be achieved between members of a school community. However,

Figure 3.1 A lexicon for analysing the flows of power in organizations

---

A   The bureaucratic framework

Formal and informal elements of an organization's structures – perhaps shown in an organizational diagram
Culture: official norms, values, beliefs – enshrined in its vision and sense of mission which are manifested through the rites, rituals and customs of a school
Power: authority/influence
Arenas and networks of negotiation:
        Formal   – meetings 'cycle'
                    – noticeboards
                    – electronic communication
        Informal   – in time and/or space
                    – related to social activities
                    – electronic communication

Bases of power:
        post of responsibility (formal and informal)
        coalitions/interest groups/factions (formal and informal)

B   The interactive aspects

Staff and students' interests:
        professional – institutional, technical/curriculum
        personal – technical/curriculum, work-oriented, social
Interests of other stakeholders in the school
Strategies of power and the rates of exchange for negotiation
Culture: groups and subgroups of participants of and in a school constructing shared values with other members of their communities of practice; individuals' views, values and beliefs
Sources of power: professional and personal (for institutional see bases, above)
Processes of power: influence

---

collegial cultures are said by the school improvement movement to be essential for bringing about change successfully (Hopkins 2001) because they reflect particular social and educational values that promote participation by members in decision-making and engagement with learning.

The construction of organizational cultures takes place within but also influences the framework of asymmetrical power relationships that occur in hierarchical organizations, such as schools. These are asymmetrical because some people, such as middle leaders, hold promoted posts in the formal organization of a school and so have greater access to some sources of power than other people. They can gain this access through a variety of micro-political strategies (Busher 2001) and use it to influence decisions and promote their own preferred value positions and solutions. Ribbins (1999) argues that all decision-making in schools involves political acts that encompass value-laden choices involving moral, financial and personnel judgements about different courses of action. Where leaders use their access to power to manipulate people to their own ends rather than to facilitate the engagement of colleagues in decision-making processes, Hargreaves (1994) describes such cultures pejoratively as ones of contrived collegiality. Busher and Saran (1992) noted in their study that such tactics by leaders fairly rapidly led to cynicism about and non-engagement in school decision-making by other staff members.

Construing power

Power is the means not only by which people assert their preferred values and choices over those of other people, but also the means by which they prevent other people making choices or, indeed, challenge the choices that have already been implemented, perhaps by controlling the agenda for discussion (Lukes 1974). It is often perceived as having two main forms, that of authority arising from the offices in a formal organization that people hold, and that arising from influence that comes from people's personal and professional skills and knowledge (Bacharach and Lawler 1980). It is available to people from a variety of sources (see Tables 3.1 and 3.2, pages 35 and 36). Bacharach and Lawler (1980) outline several different sources of power that people can access while French and Raven (1968) present a different typology. Bennett (2001) offers yet another typology (see Table 3.2), while Torres (1999: 99) suggests there are five sources of power: 'physical force, the basis of coercion; control of necessary material resources, the basis for domination; the strength of the better argument, the basis for influence; the capacity to deliberately misrepresent, the basis for manipulation; and advantageous location within a system of meanings, the basis of authority.

Power arises through the quality of interpersonal interactions in an organization which some, such as Parsons (1986), compare to a process of exchange. Foucault (1986) takes a less mechanistic perspective, perceiving power 'as something which circulates, or rather as something which only functions in the form of a chain' (p. 234). It is not, therefore, an item in itself that can be picked off a shelf. Power cannot be accessed unless people engage in dialogue and action with other people and with the social and organizational systems that these people singly and in groups or coalitions constitute. Interaction may be dispositional and latent but if there is none, whether face to face or at a distance, there is no flow of power. Power cannot be projected successfully unless those being led give their consent, whether that is derived willingly or by coercion. Willingness, however, has many shades to it as Wolcott (1977) perceived in his description of followers' responses to leaders' actions, from that of enthusiastic support to outright opposition. Coercion can take many forms, too. Allix (2000) points out that

Table 3.1 Different sources of power available to teacher middle leaders

Bacharach and Lawler (1980)	Weber (1947)	Busher (1992)
POWER can be subdivided into AUTHORITY (which is related to formal social and organizational structures) and INFLUENCE (which is related to a variety of personal attributes)	FORMAL AUTHORITY is related to hierarchical office (organizational structures) and gives legitimacy to people's actions, while FUNCTIONAL AUTHORITY arises from technical knowledge and subsumes RATIONAL AUTHORITY. In addition people as persons have CHARISMATIC AUTHORITY to a greater or lesser degree	POWER arises for teachers in various ways from and through PERSONAL QUALITIES, e.g. enthusiasm, being supportive, efficient, dependable, resilient, personal networks; PROFESSIONAL KNOWLEDGE, e.g. subject and pedagogic expertise, access to networks and information, control of students, knowledge of school system; INSTITUTIONAL HIERARCHY, e.g. formal status, access to physical and financial resources, networks to senior staff, communications

the forceful projection of particular values by somebody who, in other circumstances, might be described as a transformational leader (Burns 1978) can be as coercive as more obvious physical or financial means (Etzioni 1961).

Power not only resides in the actions and interactions of individuals, it also resides with groups or collectivities of people who hold particular expectations of socially patterned cultural activities (Lukes 1974). So some sources of power are located in formal institutional systems linked, perhaps, to particular offices (Busher 2001), while others are located outside an organization with particular collectivities that can be influential in it. Yet others are represented by the norms and values projected by collectivities of people in an organization, such as a work group or a department in the formal organization of a school, or in informal factions (interest groups) or networks. Leaders have to be aware of and negotiate with the expectations held of them by their colleagues and students, as well as of those held by senior staff in a school, if they are to gain and retain the consent of the people with whom they are working.

Power is not only accessible to those with formal posts in (educational) organizations, but to everybody, although it is likely to take different forms depending on people's formal status – see Table 3.3 (page 37). Wolcott (1977) points out how people who are resistant to actions by leaders may act in various ways to press their point of view. Hoyle (1981) argued that

Table 3.2 Power (authority and influence) can be derived from various resources

French and Raven (1968)	Hoyle (1981)	Morgan (1986)	Bennett (2001)
Physical power	**Head teachers have/can offer:**	**Leaders have:** formal authority;	**From access to:**
Resources power	material resources;	control of scarce resources; use of	Physical power
Position power	promotion; esteem; to	organizational structures, rules,	Economic power
Expert power	delegate autonomy; to vary	regulations; control of decision	Administrative knowledge
Personal (referent) power	the use of rules	processes; control of symbolism and	Technical knowledge
	Teachers can offer:	meaning; charisma;	
	esteem; support; conformity; reputation; opinion; leadership	control of knowledge and information; control of boundaries; control of technology; can limit uncertainty; personal networks; control of informal organization	Normative definitions of (acceptable) action

power is accessible not only to those with promoted posts in educational organizations. Teachers, too, wield power as leaders in the classroom, not only through their expert knowledge in the classroom and their control of the processes of teaching and learning, but also through the authority derived from their formal position as appointed teachers in a school undertaking a job acknowledged by society as important for its continuance (Bourdieu and Passeron 1977). Students also wield power by, for example, withholding cooperation from teachers, and use it to assert their own preferred agenda and values as far as they can within the existing school system (Willis 1977).

The notions of power, authority and influence, although often used interchangeably, offer different understandings of which sources of power are most closely linked to formal institutional systems. Bacharach and Lawler (1980) use the first as a global term for the other two, distinguishing authority from influence by describing the former as legitimate power. Weber (1947) perceived authority as being of three types, two of which – rational–legal sources that underpin and are constructed through organizations (bureaucracies) and traditional sources that are embedded in the customs, norms and practices of communities – are expressions of the

Table 3.3 Sources of power available to people of different formal status

PERSONAL	PROFESSIONAL	INSTITUTIONAL
Enthusiastic	External contacts	Authority/status
Warm/supportive	Subject expertise (middle leader)	Cross-institutional links
Efficient/well organized	Pedagogic expertise (middle leader)	Access to resources
Dependable	Manages pupils effectively	Access to decision-making
Authoritative/Esteem	Links with senior colleagues	Access to external authority (middle leader)
Tough negotiator (middle leader)	Part of the (department) team	Prestige of the department (middle leader)
Interpersonal skills (middle leader)	Access to information	Focal point of communication (middle leader)
Person-oriented leadership style (middle leader)	Knowledge of school system	Control of time (middle leader)
	Alertness to change in contexts (middle leader)	Influence over culture (middle leader)
	Contacts with external agencies (middle leader)	Management of staff (middle leader)

(source: Busher 1992)

legitimate power to which Bacharach and Lawler (1980) refer. Leaders, including teachers, have access to a variety of sources of power including the authority of their office (Watson 1969), a delegated authority that is tied to their position in an institutional hierarchy, material resources provided through their institution, and cultural resources linked to the vision/ mission projected by the senior staff of the school as well as their work-related knowledge and personal sources of power.

Influence, on the other hand, arises from people's personal and professional qualities (Bacharach and Lawler 1980) and the nature of the interpersonal relationships that they construct. These arise from the knowledge that they develop as well as the personalities that they and other people hold. Giddens (1991) points out the importance of people's personal self-identities to the ways in which they interact socially. Understanding relevant knowledge, be it academic knowledge of a subject, or knowledge of how a school system works or knowledge of people as individuals and collectivities, gives some people greater access to power than others and privileges some actions over others (Foucault 1976). This book chooses to sustain the distinction between authority and influence in order to preserve clarity between what sources of power are accessible to people through the formal organizational systems within which they work and those that arise through their own personal and professional qualities.

Influence and authority are available to leaders at all levels from a variety of sources. Access to some sources of authority are delegated. For senior leaders this delegation of authority comes from school governing bodies or owners. For middle leaders, teachers and support staff it comes from senior staff to allow them to enact their position in the school hierarchy. Students, too, can be delegated authority, for example to chair a school's council or captain a football team. These sources include systemic sources (related to the hierarchical organization of the school as an institution) and material sources (disposition and allocation of finance, space, time, physical artefacts and staff). They give rise to the distributed leadership to which Gronn (2000) refers. Other sources of power are related to people's (whether staff or students or parents) personal and work-related knowledge, whatever form that takes, and are referred to as influence. These might be described as symbolic, social, personal (or charismatic), technical or pedagogical (related to teaching and learning) and epistemological (knowledge of knowledge structures and the curriculum). Some of these, especially the symbolic, through which people project their vision and values for their school communities or sub-communities of pastoral and subject areas, or Key Stage areas, might give rise to transformational leadership (Burns 1978).

A case study: being a middle leader – drawing on evidence

This section is based on a study undertaken in 2001/2002 and first presented in part at a British Educational Research Association conference in 2002 (Busher 2002). The particular external policy contexts for these middle leaders were those of some English secondary schools in the early twenty-first century. The influence of these contexts on internal policy processes is discussed more fully in Chapter 2. The work of middle leaders, as the term suggests, lies at the middle of the hierarchies of their institutions, managing subject and pastoral departments or services departments, such as site maintenance or clerical work (Busher and Saran 1995), the policy frameworks of which are shaped by their senior staff as well as external socio-political contexts to create a framework for action for people – students, staff, parents – in each school. 'The [SMT] influence through things like the school improvement plan, the school aims of teaching and learning ... whole school policies, changes and targets' (female head of geography).

Although middle leaders are delegated authority by senior staff to carry out their functions when they are appointed, they are only able to operate successfully with the consent of their colleagues. So middle leaders have to be acutely aware of the differing and sometimes conflicting demands on them by senior staff and departmental colleagues, as is shown in Table 3.1. How middle leaders meet these expectations reflects the social and educational values they hold, which in turn affects the cultures they construct with their colleagues in their departments, the repertoire of micro-political strategies they deploy more or less appropriately, and their ability to access and apply a variety of sources of power to create and enact policy. Thus the attempt to construct particular cultures or sub-cultures for departments is part of the political process of asserting some values over others in order to carry out the necessary core work of a school of learning supported by the most appropriate forms of teaching possible.

Some sources of authority for middle leaders

The institutional systems in which middle leaders work allows them access to a variety of sources of power, because of their roles in their institution (see Table 3.3), to help them implement departmental policies that are approved by the senior staff of a school. The three main sources of this institutional power are: delegated authority, systemic support for action and material resources to implement approved policies. Access to these sources of power is conditional on having tacit or explicit approval for action from senior staff. Tacit approval comes when middle leaders' actions arise from the normal remit of their job – often indicated in a job specification or in subsequent developments of that through discussions with senior staff. Explicit approval comes from direct and usually recent discussions with senior staff about policy implementation at departmental level. This might take the form of personal discussions between senior and middle leaders either individually or as part of a discussion in one of the school's decision-making arenas, such as a meeting of heads of departments. Having access to sources of authority supported by senior staff, who embody the school system (Foucault 1986), means that middle leaders have to act as agents for the senior staff.

Delegated authority
Although they do not revel in making manifest their authority of office (a delegated authority), middle leaders are keenly aware of it and claim they are willing to use it when necessary to project senior staff policy and their own departmental policy as a sub-set of that. As part of the process of policy implementation they act as buffers between senior staff and departmental colleagues by, for example, thinking through the implications of senior management policy before presenting it to their departments and pointing

out to colleagues which aspects of policy can be modified and which have to be sustained. When departmental colleagues disagree with senior staff policies or the manner of their implementation, middle leaders act as conduits of information between senior staff and departmental colleagues to try to construct a compromise path of action, but some participants, the more powerful senior staff, are more likely to be satisfied with the outcomes than others.

Middle leaders' delegated authority, however, also gives them access to arenas of discussion not open to non-promoted staff, for example formal arenas such as a school's middle leaders' forum, as well as giving them the privilege of talking with senior staff privately about school-wide decisions. Their access to and their support from senior staff allow middle leaders to assert their agenda on policy when negotiating with departmental colleagues. 'It almost gives it more validity if [colleagues] know that I have been talking to [SMT] … it is not just me implementing something' (male head of RE).

This association with formal institutional sources of power also affected their implementation of practice in the same manner. For example, because senior staff in one school wanted students' marks recorded in a certain way at a certain time – a practice with which several middle leaders in this school seemed to agree in order to monitor student progress – middle leaders put pressure on their colleagues to meet the deadlines set by senior staff. 'Getting information on the computer. Reports sorted out … assessments at the right time; books marked; meeting requirements for teaching and everything that goes with it' (male humanities teacher).

Access to power via delegated authority also gave middle leaders access to coercion – in this case not physical threats but fear of losing senior staff approval if certain requests were not complied with through certain actions by a certain time.

This delegated authority was most visibly projected through the series of formal meetings that middle leaders held. As they were chaired by the middle leaders and decisions from the meetings were followed up by them, that authority was clearly embodied (Foucault 1977) and the asymmetrical power relationships of the department made obvious. 'We have a formal briefing every Thursday morning and then we have a faculty meeting once every four or five weeks on a Monday afternoon after school for an hour. But the actual real running takes place constantly throughout the day, breaks, lunch times and during lessons' (male humanities teacher).

Middle leaders claimed these meetings generated a sense of ownership of departmental policies among colleagues because 'they have the opportunity to comment and if they have chosen not to do that they have to play the system' (female head of geography). How genuine was this sense of ownership is hard to determine although there was some evidence from conversations with other colleagues of the middle leaders that they felt the meetings were an opportunity for genuine consultation even if they acknowledged that decision-making ultimately lay with the middle leader. They did not portray the cynicism encountered by Busher and Saran (1992) among teachers who had experienced consultation as merely a charade to cover senior staff decisions.

Middle leaders also used their authority of office (Watson 1969) when balancing the competing demands of colleagues, for example insisting that colleagues not only signed out resources taken from a stock cupboard, but also returned them and shelved them tidily at the end of lessons for the good of whichever colleague needed to use them next.

Systemic support for action

Middle leaders make use of their formal status to access the authority vested in their institution by its governing body and/or owners (or the state, if a public school) to implement effective education. For example, where staff colleagues face problems in controlling students who are perceived as difficult, middle leaders take action to support them, whether this is to intervene and discipline the student or to help the teacher take appropriate action themselves. One teacher in this study reported referring students who misbehaved in her lessons to her subject leader who disciplined them by speaking to them – making manifest his authority over the student – then using a local form of punishment called faculty report, as well as making visible the students' misdemeanours to people whom they might see as their significant others, their parents, by sending a letter home.

In another case a middle leader acted to support a relatively inexperienced teacher to develop and organize a field trip, helping her to scope the fieldwork first of all, then helping her to gain the support of senior staff for the implementation of the fieldwork. When, having given their approval in principle for the fieldwork to go ahead, the senior staff changed their minds and decided to cancel the visit, the middle leader went to see the senior staff to argue the case for it, explaining how important it was for the development of effective learning by students for this particular topic in the curriculum. She also referred to the views of external inspectors of the school as justification for the fieldwork. When the fieldwork was then again given permission by the senior staff to take place, the middle leader showed the teacher the range of safety procedures that had to be implemented, how to arrange transport, and how to proceed with getting parents' permission for their children's involvement in it.

Material resources

Another form through which middle leaders demonstrated their delegated authority was through their access to material resources, especially where they were budget holders for their departments. Middle leaders made available a variety of resources to colleagues, not merely those that they were able to purchase to support the curriculum. For example, in one department the middle leader provided teachers with 'a folder of all the assessments and the scheme of work and all the various work sheets for different abilities [of students] ... a video list, what videos are where and when I can show them ... on the wall there is a sheet where we can book the textbooks out' (female RE teacher).

Although budget allocations reflected middle leaders' moral and professional values and dilemmas, they were also said by their colleagues to reflect the cultural norms established in the departments and to be taken collaboratively. Some middle leaders talked about the problems of negotiating with senior staff to get the budgets they needed to implement the curriculum innovations that they wanted to improve the quality of learning and teaching.

Sources of influence

Sources of influence (or informal power) used by middle leaders arise from their personal and professional knowledge and skills (see Table 3.3). The former are manifested in the interpersonal relationships and departmental cultures that middle leaders helped to establish (see below). The latter took the form of knowledge resources, symbolic resources and rewards, and negotiative skills (politics of compromise and the performance of advocacy) which helped their colleagues to cope with the school organization in which they worked and acknowledged their achievement in doing so. The last they displayed through micro-political strategies they used.

Creating organizational cultures and sub-cultures as a source of influence
Lenski (1986) points out how ruling elites may unobtrusively emphasize existing norms or construct new rules to legitimate certain actions and processes in society to retain their control more efficiently than by coercing people, a process similar to that used by senior management teams and teachers in schools to frame school processes and regulations that require people to act in particular ways and leave unchallenged their control. Lukes (1974), citing Bacharach and Baratz, perceives this as a mobilization of bias so that certain rules, beliefs and rituals are brought into being which only legitimate certain courses of action that favour a particular perspective, that upheld by the ruling leaders or managers. Hardy (1985) argues that such use of unobtrusive power creates attitudes among subordinate groups and individuals that allow the powerful to endow their actions or proposed actions with legitimacy in the eyes of those people. This is less costly and corrosive of social cohesion than is the repeated use of coercion (Lenski 1986). School cultures and departmental sub-cultures are examples of this construction of norm frameworks that shape action and are therefore a form of influence for those who construct them or have a major influence in shaping them.

The cultures that middle leaders construct in their departments reflect the personal and professional values that they develop through time as well as those of their colleagues. The values come from a variety of sources: their family backgrounds or their personal interests; teachers with whom they had come into contact as students either at school or in higher education; teachers with whom they had worked early in their careers (Busher 2005a).

Middle leaders in this study espoused professional values that focused on building collaborative but toughly purposeful cultures within the asymmetrical power relationships that existed in their institutions. All the middle leaders believed the curriculum subjects they and their colleagues in their departments taught were important and so were keen to get students engaged with them, believing this would help them to develop as people, as well as helping their departments meet their targets of pass rates of students in public examinations.

Middle leaders tried to create socially cohesive departments because they thought these would help colleagues to work together successfully to improve teaching and learning. So they encouraged colleagues to collaborate with them in curriculum development so the whole team had ownership of it (male head of history). Such a culture was built on 'teamwork, mutual trust, and academic and professional respect' (male head of history). Although middle leaders being supportive of their colleagues' work (female history teacher) was an important element, so too was middle leaders' ability to 'deliver criticism with a smile' (male humanities teacher) when necessary because teachers needed 'to feel when they are not doing it right that they are accountable but none the less valued and supported' (female history teacher). In one case this sense of community was contrasted sharply with life in a department under a former middle leader (male humanities teacher).

These sub-cultures gave middle leaders considerable esteem among their colleagues, encouraging the latter to follow their lead, but also constraining middle leaders, if they were not to generate cynicism, by defining the ways in which they might act and take decisions, showing again how power is held by collectivities as well as by individuals (Lukes 1974).

Knowledge resources as sources of influence

A major source of middle leaders' influence is their professional knowledge (see Table 3.3). Mortimore (1993) categorized this as knowledge of curriculum, pedagogy, social and psychological processes, and organizational systems and policy processes. Teachers and senior staff thought that middle leaders had greater subject knowledge than others in their departments, although some middle leaders themselves disputed this ascription. They were also said to have expert pedagogic knowledge on how to manage aspects of the curriculum and how to manage students. They were also said to and expected to have knowledge of organizational processes. For example, one teacher admired his head of department's 'very good knowledge of how things work and who to approach ... She seems to know protocol very well ... the right people to go and talk to and in what order ... on writing schemes of work. She has given me practical tips on how to file' (male humanities teacher). In another department teachers admired the subject leader because he was 'a very good strategic planner and manager of things' (female history teacher).

Symbolic resources and rewards as sources of influence

Middle leaders draw on their personal and professional values and knowledge to develop symbolic understandings of the purposes of their departments, creating a sense of vision for the department that, for these middle leaders, focused on how they might best serve the needs of students. Although this seemed to involve accepting colleagues' suggestions about how to implement that vision, nevertheless it seemed to contain elements of coercion, as Allix (2000) suggested it might:

> The bottom line is I am head of faculty and this is how we are going to do it, like it or not ... Nowhere in the faculty do we work in isolation. We don't all have our little worksheets that we keep secret. It is a team thing. We have central resources and common schemes of work ... monitored to see how different classes are doing and that staff are meeting deadlines ...
>
> (female head of humanities)

Other symbols that middle leaders projected were the importance of having successful departments and colleagues being members of those. Success was usually represented in terms of public examination results but also in terms of having interesting approaches to teaching. This included having access to and having accessible a wide range of teaching and learning resources which people could share within and through an administrative framework. Middle leaders appealed to their colleagues to sustain these symbols by collaborating to enact them. Pastoral departments portrayed success differently, in terms of student achievement rather than attainment and in terms of students' personal and social development and engagement in school activities – often displayed in photographs.

Negotiative resources as sources of influence

Middle leaders acknowledged that not all their ideas and suggested policies were a success, and some were costly because of the resistance they encountered which was possibly corrosive of the culture of collegiality that they cared for. Resistance, here, encompasses those views held reasonably by other people that stand in opposition to those of the (middle) leaders. Such views are not necessarily better or worse than those of the leaders but contradicted them. Sometimes the people holding them are in less powerful positions bureaucratically to implement or sustain this oppostion, but at other times they are more powerful. Resistance can occur for various reasons, as Plant (1987) explained – see Figure 3.2.

Figure 3.2 Possible causes of resistance to change

Fear of the unknown	Poor relationships
Misinformation	Fear of failure
Historical factors	Fear of looking stupid
Threats to cores skills and competence	Reluctance to experiment
Threats to status	Custom bound
Threat to power base	Reluctance to let go
No perceived benefits	Strong peer group norms
Low-trust organizational climate	

(source: Plant 1987)

Wolcott (1977) offers an interesting continuum of different approaches that people take to engaging in resistance, from outright confrontation to merely engaging reluctantly in actions. As van der Westhuizen (1996) pointed out, conflict is endemic in institutions and is a normal part of social life, not a pathological manifestation of poor management, reflecting the variety of different views and values that people bring to their work. It is how such conflicts are resolved that is of key importance to sustaining positive interpersonal processes. Table 3.4 (page 46) offers some possible suggestions.

In the case of these middle leaders, conflicts seemed to have led to further rounds of negotiation. Conflict turned out to be a creative rather than a destructive force when handled in particular ways. 'You have to know the character of the department. Sometimes things don't go down very well at all. You have to listen to what they are saying, and sometimes that is fine because it could be about workload, which is a real issue' (female head of humanities).

Middle leaders' greatest dilemmas came when senior staff policy demands were in conflict with the interests and views of their departmental colleagues. To limit the potential damage of such policies to themselves and their departmental colleagues, while none the less sustaining the interests of the senior staff from whom their delegated authority came, middle leaders tried to mediate the implementation of this policy so that their departmental colleagues gained some control of its processes.

Table 3.4 Coping with resistance

PROBLEMS	STRATEGIES
(False) perceptions of colleagues/ non-communication	Try to draw the department together; help professional competence and personal understanding Improve a person's sense of self-esteem Isolate 'the cancer' Point out the impact of department disunity on department image Use senior staff to re-open negotiation
Personal and/or principled conflict; senior staff don't welcome change; don't disturb other staff	Making 'monkeys' comfortable Managing change from below The cultural pincers of 'proper conduct' Pressures from external contexts (e.g. exam results) Enticing people out of bunkers
Fear from the past/past wounds/ 'the conservative'	Personal discussion Use an outside facilitator Ignore them, outflank them, INSET, lock into their perceptions, provide a mirror Personal contact, open discussion, agreeing differences, acknowledging strengths

'We'll agree that [in the faculty] … whilst they may not have any say in what is happening, they will have some say about how it is going to be implemented within our own department … so it is best for us, so [we] do have some ownership' (female head of humanities).

To achieve this, middle leaders often acted as advocates (Bradley and Roaf 1995) for their colleagues to senior staff, seeking a compromise on means of policy implementation if not on the actual policy itself. This was a central part of the Janus-faced work of middle leaders through which they demonstrated to their departmental colleagues that they were still part of the departmental team and not just the messengers for senior staff. Gunter *et al.* (2001) comment on the strains that middle leaders experience because of their location organizationally at the interface between junior and senior staff.

This seems to be evidence of what Burns (1978) described as transactional leadership – people bartering with colleagues to get the best outcomes possible rather than their initial preferred outcomes. Another example of this was of one middle leader negotiating with colleagues when allocating classes at the start of a school year. In his view it was likely to produce more successful teaching – and more satisfied teachers – if, as far as possible, he allocated teachers to the classes they preferred, always making sure that through time everybody took an equitable load of more and less difficult groups of students to teach.

A third example is of middle leaders drawing on knowledge or support that comes from outside the school organization. When this is legitimated by socially recognized bodies in the macro-culture of a school, such as professional societies or OFSTED, it gives middle leaders access to sources of dispersed power that can, in some cases, allow middle leaders to 'over-trump' the views and policies of senior staff, and challenge successfully the decisions they have made.

Some possible research agenda

- How is power distributed in your school?
- What are the main sources of power and influence that you notice people using in your institution (apply this to students and support staff as well as to teachers and people holding promoted posts in the organizational hierarchy)?
- What are considered admissible and inadmissible uses of power in your school or college?
- How is power constructed by different groups as well as individuals?
- How is power used by different people or groups to pursue their interests and those of others, as well as to resist other people's agenda?

4 School leaders as politicians
Governing in whose interests?

Leaders as rulers

The construction of schools as organizations and communities is carried out by all participants in a school, be they students, teachers, support staff or governors, but some people have more access to power to influence the shaping of these entities. The more powerful are usually the formally designated senior leaders of a school, who try to enact a variety of policies in particular socio-economic and macro-policy contexts to construct preferred organizational cultures and teaching and learning practices. It involves the creating, organizing, managing, monitoring and resolving of value conflicts of many different people which reflects the view of the world constructed by each member of a school. Leadership is carried out at many levels in a school from senior leaders (head teachers or deputies) to middle leaders, who manage academic and pastoral departments as well as administrative services such as the school office or the school site, to first-line leaders or supervisors. They are whose authority to act in certain socially defined ways in certain circumstances (e.g. lessons) or social arenas (such as classrooms or playgrounds) to supervise other people is based on their hierarchical position in a school. There are, however, also informal leaders, whether at school, department or classroom level or in extra-mural activities, whose influence is based more on their personal and work-related skills and knowledge and their alliances with other people inside and outside school than on their formal position in a school. Among such people might be students as well as teachers.

From this, Muijs and Harris (2003) have developed the concept of teacher leaders, people who have a major part of their work based in the classroom but seek to work collectively with their colleagues outside it to shape school policy. Katzenmeyer and Moller (2001), admittedly writing in an American context, also emphasize the importance of classroom practice as a defining criteria for teacher leaders. Not surprisingly, then, Frost and Durrant (2003) firmly confine the notion of teacher leadership to people holding non-promoted posts in schools but who take a lead in decision-making in a school beyond the doors of their classrooms. They argue that this is presenting an alternative understanding to hierarchically based conceptions of leadership, disregarding the impossibility of having institutions without asymmetrical power relationships, and therefore hierarchies.

From this perspective people, not systems, are the centres of knowing and the constructors of meaning (Harrison 1994: 177). So institutions and communities like schools (Sergiovanni 1994) are built through processes of debate, dialogue and interaction between individuals and between individuals and collectivities, such as departments or groups of students or, occasionally, groups of parents. The discourses of these different groups are shaped by the asymmetrical power relationships that exist between different members of a school but reflect their members' preferred values and perspectives which, in turn, reflect their interpretations of various national and local policy imperatives, and lead to the implementation of approaches to teaching and learning that are consonant with their views. For example, although staff in many schools claim to support democracy, few schools are run on democratic lines and teachers in most schools are more concerned in practice with educational outcomes like examination results than with the personal and social development of students, especially of those who are marginal to the school community in various ways. It leads Ribbins (1999) to argue that making decisions over which actions to pursue, since only some can be implemented, involves moral and political choices in which sets of overt or covert values are embedded and as a result of which resources are allocated to some people and projects rather than to others.

Leaders at all levels in schools, as in other communities in society, try to circumvent the dilemmas and social tensions they generate by creating what they claim are rational processes and rules for taking decisions which legitimate their decisions. These rules legitimate certain actions and processes and require people to act in particular ways (Lenski 1986), so helping leaders to retain their control more efficiently than by coercing people. Constructing rule frameworks for communities so their members police themselves (Foucault 1977) is less corrosive of social cohesion than leaders directly confronting and coercing colleagues or subordinates. Thus members of a community become complicit with their leaders in monitoring their own constraint.

Control of the rules of a society or organization for constructing action and organizational systems is a powerful means of exerting influence or sustaining dominance by a group, such as the governors or senior management team of a school. The rules shaping how decisions are made in an organization are distinct from the social and organizational systems themselves, the former providing the means for constructing and sustaining the latter. Giddens (1984) argues that people have to assert their agency against both the rules (structures) and the systems. When members of a community or sub-community transgress the rules set up by powerful people in them, leaders, like head teachers and middle managers, employ sanctions to coerce them into compliance (Etzioni 1961). These sanctions can take many forms apart from physical threats, such as denial of access to material and symbolic resources, withdrawal of privileges offered by the system, and exclusion from normal processes of communication and consultation.

Decision-making in schools, then, including the processes of teaching and learning, can be perceived as political and negotiative interactions that are invested with flows of power through the people taking part in them. A possible configuration of this model is shown in Figure 4.1.

Level 1 of Figure 4.1 is discussed in Chapter 3. Level 2 maps the range of pressure groups to be found in a school, both those that are formally constituted as part of the organizational system of a school, such as subject or pastoral departments or Key Stage sections of a school, and informal ones.

Figure 4.1 Main political features of a school organization

Level 1: Manifestations of power			
Authority (formal power)	**Influence (informal power)**	**Bases**	**Sources**
▼	▼	▼	▼
Headship v. leadership (Gibb 1947)		Organizational structure; rites, rituals, customs; interest groups/factions	Institutional; work-related; personal
Level 2: Organizational groups and coalitions			
(overlapping membership)			
Formal organizational (interest) groups		**Factions[2] (informal interest groups)**	**Networks (pressure groups)**
▼		▼	▼
Standing,[1] e.g. subject department; ad hoc,[1] e.g. working parties; cross-institutional [[1]Poster (1976)]		Work-related; social [[2]Hoyle (1982) – interest sets] [Burns (1955) – cliques/cabals]	Work-related; social
Level 3: Processes of negotiations			
Social framework		**Strategies**	**Sites and locations**
▼		▼	▼
Norms, values, beliefs; rates of exchange; people's and groups' interests		Bureaucratic; interactive; resistant	Arenas, e.g. meetings (formal and informal); electronic networks (personal and professional)

(source: Busher 2001)

The informal groups will also have a recognizable membership. They may be formed around curriculum-related activities, such as school sports teams or dramatic or musical activities, and may contain elements of social activity among their members – as might the formal groups, too. Another nexus for such interest groups are staff activities, such as cricket or football teams. Less formal still, and usually related to activities outside a school, are those networks of staff, or indeed students, who meet out of school for various activities, for example, sport or religious activities. All these groups have particular interests – see Table 4.1 on page 54 for some examples – and members are likely to sustain or press forward those interests during any negotiations. They might, for example, try to preserve the integrity of a particular period of time after school for their activities, or lobby gatekeepers of school physical, financial and symbolic resources for access to those.

Level 3 indicates the sites through which people negotiate as well as the range of strategies available to people – see Table 4.2 on page 59 for some examples of these – and the constructed norms within that community or school organization that usually underpin such negotiations. However, this is not to pursue a Parsonian (Parsons 1986) view of power as essentially a transactional process of exchange but merely to mark some of the cultural norms that shape the flows of power in organizations (Foucault 1977), such as the construction of organizational rules and procedures that privilege some discussions and points of view and not others.

The sites of negotiation range from formal arenas, such as heads of departments' meetings, or school governors' meetings, through informal arenas where people may meet by chance or contrivance over coffee, for example, on a regular basis, to chance meetings in corridors. Such analysis can be applied equally to the range of sites used by students for their negotiations and discussions. Skilled leaders among staff and students know where and when such formal and informal arenas exist in their institutions and learn to use them appropriately. The more informal arenas serve usefully to sound out opinion before discussions emerge into the formal arenas of formal school meetings where people may be unwilling to give up established positions because of the implications it might have for their perceived persona.

It is at this point that the moral dilemmas of power emerge. Fullan (2001) as well as Hodgkinson (1991) consider leadership to be essentially a moral art, facing post-holders constantly with moral dilemmas about which decisions to take, since taking one set of decisions is likely to exclude others, privileging some people's needs over others. MacBeath and MacDonald (2000) suggest that ethical decision-making, which takes transparent account of the needs of other members of a school community, is key to how school leaders use power successfully since it promotes social cohesion and creates more accessible teaching and learning opportunities for all students. Developing school cultures and departmental sub-cultures that foster positive interpersonal relationships based on shared values helps people to construct a sense of community (Sergiovanni 1992, 2001). A key element of such cultures is that of trust between members. This, Smyth *et al.* (2000) claim, is most likely to sustain a critical dialogue about the practices of teaching and learning and the development of those to better meet the needs of all students. Gronn (2000) suggests it leads to a genuine distribution of leadership that will promote the personal and work-related growth of staff, students and parents.

Governing in whose interests? Enacting school leadership for whose utopian future?

At the centre of leaders' dilemmas is the quandary of making choices about whose values they enact and in whose interests. Part of this tension relates to their own sense of self-identity that they have created to sustain them in their professional careers. Part of it relates to the educational and social values that they hold. Part of it relates to the powerful contexts and the distributions of power in those contexts that they perceive putting pressure on their choices in education. Part of it relates to their views of the colleagues and students with whom they work most closely and who form an integral part of their main social and professional communities.

The pursuit and enactment of self-identity by people is a central aspect of their development of agency (Giddens 1991). Greenfield (1993) perceives this process as being made up of acts of individual will and practice, an existential view according to Ryan (2003). Giddens (1984) construes it as part of an interactive process in which people engage with other people to construct social systems and structures. The notion of identity derives from where and how people locate themselves within a society or a community (LaFontaine 1985; Bourdieu 1990), as well as from the Greek notion of persona or mask that allows people to play particular parts in a community, whether or not it is a fictional one on a stage (Hollis 1985).

So the notion of developing personhood (Aubrey *et al.* 2000), in which all people continuously engage, is complex, made up of individual and social elements and, in the contexts of institutionalized work, of elements that are related to a person's work-related life and elements that are not. The latter are often not visible to work-based colleagues. People develop their work-related (professional) self-identities through their interactions with other people in a variety of milieux through time. These identities are grounded in people's individual histories, personalities and work-related experiences (Nias 1999; Measor and Sikes 1992; Thomas 1995), including, for staff in schools, their experiences as students in various institutions (e.g. Gersten 1995). Students and staff use dialogic and reflective ways to develop their professional or work-related selves (Schon 1987) and the core educational and social values to guide their actions consciously and unconsciously (Hodgkinson 1991; Begley 1999a).

Leaders and middle leaders – following current nomenclature in England (Bennett *et al.* 2003) for heads of academic and pastoral departments and Key Stage curriculum leaders in schools – and other staff and students in schools and colleges are driven by personal and work-related values by which they define what they consider to be 'good' practice. Often, of course, individuals may be unaware of the deeply held assumptions upon which these values are based and cannot therefore articulate them clearly. These views may or may not be in conflict with those policies projected at national, local and institutional level by people holding powerful offices at these different levels of school governance, such as senior leaders in schools. Further, the values that individual staff in a school hold may or may not be in conflict with those of other teachers and support staff or with those of students and their parents. Thrupp (1999) and O'Connor (1997), among many others, point out how the socio-economic background of students (the school mix) affects the ways in which schools are managed and perform academically. Osler *et al.* (2000) point to conflicts between students' expectations of schooling and teachers' views as a cause of student disaffection that often leads to student exclusion. Vincent (2000) discusses how getting parents involved in supporting the curriculum can improve the quality of students' performances.

To implement their preferred values, policies and practices, leaders have to gain access to and use power, but they cannot do this unless they engage in dialogue and action with other people singly or in groups within and outside a school's social and organizational systems. This interaction is carried out through a repertoire of micro-political strategies that Ball (1987) perceives as the means by which people try to implement their own preferred educational and social values and practices by gaining access to the necessary resources.

Many of these micro-political strategies can be learnt through working with other people and observing other people at work. Teachers use a variety of different micro-political strategies, such as creating variety in their lessons or enforcing particular patterns of student behaviour to guide students' learning and keep control of their lessons. Some of these are linked to the authority delegated to them by their school whereas others flow from their personal or work-related knowledge and skills (Busher 2001). In some circumstances these are used to transform or reproduce existing social and curriculum relationships between staff and students or to resist change and pursue their particular work-related interests – see Table 4.1. Such strategies have also been identified and explored by Loveless (1999) in his analysis of how attempts to move away from ability streaming in a mathematics department were thwarted by teachers in alliance with parents. Other members of a school community such as students use micro-

political strategies to position themselves in ways that are socially or organizationally advantageous to them (Benjamin 2002), allowing them to play
an esteemed part in their communities as well as achieving what they perceive as their purposes in education. Wolcott (1977) pointed out the variety
of strategies of compliance and resistance used by people in organizations.

Table 4.1 Examples of teachers' interests in school decision-making negotiations

Professional interests		Personal interests	
Institutional	*Technical/ curriculum*	*Work or career-oriented*	*Social*
Effectiveness of school organization	Preferred pedagogic styles	Career	Many and varied: how people like to spends their leisure time
		Self-esteem	
Territory – physically (e.g. which classroom) and symbolically	Preferred aspects of the curriculum to teach	Extra-curricular activities	
Prestige of the school or the subject area	Curriculum-related knowledge, e.g. assessment procedures	School or subject area culture	
		Job satisfaction	
Effectiveness of pupil discipline	Particular resources available	Relationships with colleagues and pupils	
Relationships with senior staff	Time available for teaching preferred topics or extra-curricular activities	Educational and social values	
How well time was managed – teaching timetable, meetings			
	How pupils are grouped	Quality of informal communications	

School policy and practice are contested arenas for all members of a
school, including the students, who are trying to give meaning to their
work and lives through their interactions with other people and the institutional systems that surround them. So all members of a school community perform as political actors in the arena of the whole school as well as
in those of departments and classrooms, bargaining if necessary to defend
their own curricular, pedagogical or political interests – see Table 4.1. Hase
et al. (1999) suggest that self-interest, conscious or unconscious, creates difficulties in making disinterested decisions, without noting that 'disinterested decisions' is a value-laden notion that sustains current asymmetrical
power relationships and existing organizational systems and structures,
whatever injustices they contain. Further, individuals' and groups' personal

and work-related interests are likely to reflect their principled views of what constitutes successful teaching and learning or navigating the hazards of the school day, as well as various educational and social values that they have established through time as part of their work-related identities.

Attempts to implement values and policies depend for their success on people gaining consent from others, whether other individuals or groups of people, which may be a sub-community, such as a department, in the formal organization of a school. Such individuals and collectivities can hinder the implementation of ideas and practices if their consent is not gained – as is discussed in Chapter 3. Lukes (1974) points out that power can be held by collectivities of people as well as by individuals, while Foucault (1986) suggests that although power is not held as a property by anybody, it can be accessed by a variety of people in a variety of ways be they students, staff, governors or parents.

The personal and work-related values of teachers and other more senior leaders in schools often form a coherent entity, however well or poorly articulated, that represents each individual's vision for how best to meet the social and educational needs of a wide variety of students. In some sense teachers' or leaders' visions for success are utopian (Halpin 2003). Not only do they represent a coherent conceptual and value frame-work for making sense of the world and for taking action in it but they also represent an ideal state to be worked towards that is unlikely ever to be fully implemented. As such they provide a test ground against which current policies and practices can be judged and projected changes evaluated for how well they help practitioners to advance their vision or hinder its achievement. Such visions are not always predicated on pursuit of the common good. However, such visions form part of each person's work-related self-identity, be they students, teachers, support staff or school-level leaders. What may be missing from them is an appreciation of other people's perceptions, identities and legitimately held values, particularly those less powerful than themselves. Typically in a school these are the voices of students and parents, and marginalized students and parents in particular who come from disadvantaged social backgrounds, minority ethnic backgrounds, or who have various forms of learning or behavioural difficulties that may inhibit them from contributing positively to a school's drive for an elevated position in national league tables of school perform-ance in England at present.

Micro-political strategies: engaging in action

People rarely act on their own, whether they are staff or students, seeking friends, colleagues or allies wherever they can to sustain their own preferred views of life (schooling, education). Homans (1958) and Blau

(1964) point out how people negotiate with each other to advance their own agenda. Thus coupled to understandings of how the perspec-tives and agenda of individual people influence the way they behave in organi-zations has to be understandings of how people behave in groups to achieve their agenda, i.e. how people behave politically, whether at a micro (within organizations) level or at a macro level. An important element of this is how people form alliances or coalitions, either for single issues on which they share a common perspective or on a multiplicity of issues about which they share a common view. Such coalitions can emerge in both the formal and informal processes of a school organization. For their leaders they form an important base of power which can sometimes successfully challenge decisions taken by more formally powerful members of a school.

For example, in one school a group of middle leaders banded together to challenge a contract for a new photocopier that a deputy head teacher had signed (Busher 1992). The middle leaders claimed that it was more expensive than the old contract – deducted more money from their depart-mental budgets – and altered the relationships between colleagues within their departments. Because of the costs and the system the photocopier used, the middle leaders had to police access to it by their departmental col-leagues making sharply visible their formal status as middle leaders and emphasizing relationships of hierarchy in their departmental communities that were normally carefully disguised behind the use of many informal processes of decision-making to try to sustain a sense of collegiality in each department. Further, the middle leaders now found their departmental budgets were monitored by the school administrator on a monthly basis, creating for them a stronger sense of central control over them which they had previously avoided. This shift in political and social relationships threatened the sub-cultures that middle leaders had constructed with their colleagues in their departments, and so to some extent challenged the ways of life that had emerged there.

So the middle leaders agreed to carry out a campaign to persuade the deputy head to revise the contract to reduce again the costs of photocopy-ing. This took the form of them individually going to see him to discuss the issue of the photocopier from their own departments' points of view over a period of a number of weeks before the next meeting of the senior man-agement team with the middle leaders, an important arena for school deci-sion-making, or at least for the head teacher to sound out the views of middle leaders. A week or so before this meeting the deputy head was warned that some of the middle leaders had asked the head teacher to put the issue of the photocopier on the agenda of the meeting. Recognizing the collective and individual pressure of the middle leaders, the deputy head contacted the photocopy rental company before the meeting to renegotiate the contract. So at the meeting he was able to announce when the agenda item came up for discussion, that the contract was under review, thereby taking much of the strength out of the middle leaders' resistance to the contract. However, the subsequent contract negotiations led to a considerable reduction in the costs of photocopying that had to be borne by the school departments and therefore had less of an impact on their sub-cultures, to the relief of the middle leaders.

The micro-political processes of organizations show how organizations are managed and how change may be brought about. At a common-sense level, many teachers would acknowledge the reality of this perspective, although some senior staff might dispute it, preferring to see their schools as orderly, rational places. Ball (1989), too, disputed that management and micro-politics are part of the same process, assuming, perhaps, that management is only about structural processes of function and control. However, the repertoire of styles that leaders use to negotiate decisions is important to the success of the practices they are trying to implement. For example, Blase and Blase (1994) thought the style of leadership offered by a head teacher was critical in explaining how staff responded to a situation. So a collaborative style of working is a form of micro-political strategy through which a leader meets some of the needs of staff or students, gaining, in return, involvement in or at least compliance with organizational objectives and leaders' strategies.

Hence discussion of micro-political processes in management is not just about conflict, as Ball (1987) pointed out. They are also about how people develop consensus and how leaders and managers are able to guide colleagues to achieve shared and agreed outcomes. Nor are micro-political processes the dark side of life in organizations, as Hoyle (1986) suggested, which is largely hidden from view, but the everyday stuff of it through which participants – staff, students and other stakeholders – try to implement their preferred work-related and personal agenda within the contexts in which they find themselves. The fact that it has largely remained uncharted territory is more a comment on the conceptual frameworks that researchers have brought to their attempts to understand the management of schools as organizations, than of the lived realities that staff and students experience on a daily basis.

An important group of actors in these micro-political processes are the students, whether acting on their own behalf or on behalf of others, such as teachers or parents, even if perhaps that is sometimes unwitting, as Vignette 4.1 illustrates (page 58).

Revealed here is how management activity is the outcome of micro-political pressures (head teacher's authority and values; students' attempts to gain their own agenda) and a teacher's personal beliefs, values and judgements (teacher's sense of self, and her professional judgement in specific organizational and curriculum contexts). The source of many of these values and attempts at chosen action is the external environment either in its current form or as it was historically constructed. Willis (1977), for

Vignette 4.1 Pupils as spies

June (a fictitious name) described how pupils intentionally passed on messages about what went on in teachers' lessons. This had two modes. The first, an informant mode, was when pupils proactively told teachers about incidents in other teachers' classes and teachers more or less willingly listened. The second mode was that of pupil as spy. June gave an example of how the head teacher had deliberately collected information about her teaching from pupils during their career interviews with him. He had then come to see June and asked her to alter her style of curriculum delivery. June knew of the head teacher's information gathering because, after the career interviews had finished, one of the pupils had come back into June's lesson and said, 'Mr [head teacher] actually asked me what I think about you.' June then explained how she had 'complained to the Union rep about that. I don't think it is right that teachers ask children about other teachers.'

(source: Busher 1989)

example, noted how certain groups of students from particular social backgrounds sought different outcomes from their schooling than conventional academic success.

Micro-political strategies, some of which are shown in Table 4.2, are the means by which people engage with each other formally and informally in educational institutions in their endeavours to assert their own values and views of successful work-related practice. Some are derived from people's formal roles in school and the positions they hold in a school bureaucracy. Others are derived from people's interpersonal skills and knowledge. Some are used to promote people's views and values, while others may be used mainly for resisting other people's agenda.

Governing in whose interests?

This section is drawn from a small-scale study of middle leaders (Busher 2002) in some secondary schools in the Midlands area of England. The narrative of one middle leader is used to illustrate how leaders act as politicians in particular socio-political and personal contexts. The following narrative is taken from an interview with him. The views he puts forward were corroborated by colleagues in his department, but these are not shown for the sake of space. What he talks about can be summarized as follows:

Table 4.2 Micro-political strategies of innovation and resistance

Bureaucratic – use of formal authority	Interpersonal – using informal power (influence) and manipulating the culture	Resistant
Resource control	Managing the culture	Non-involvement
Job specification change	Using networks	Colonizing meetings
Changing organizational structure	Using knowledge of the the organizational system	Proclaiming autonomy
Boundary management – internal and external	Collusion with colleagues	Reference to subject-based authority
Monitoring formal decision-making arenas	Displaying values through work	Filibustering
	Positive sum bargaining	Working to contract
Controlling information		Using external contacts to support own position
Coordinating work	Making coalitions (with powerful allies)	
Defining policy	Offering support	Sounding out opinion/ gleaning information
Reference to external authority	Giving rewards or recognition	Lobbying
Permitting		Appealing to traditional norms

(source: Busher 2001)

- contexts, personal and external
- constructing professional self-identities
- authority and influence – delegated power to create policy
- culture, norms and values – constructing learning communities
- the morality of using power
- projecting power and influence: acting in whose interests?
- struggles for self-fulfilment in particular organizational contexts.

Contexts 1: Professional history

In 1985 I was given my first opportunity to be a subject leader or middle manager, of the social science department. This complemented the history department as integrated humanities became more important in the school. It was quite an exciting prospect: starting a department from scratch. There was myself and a colleague who taught psychology and sociology who set up the framework of that department, which has now grown to have three full-time staff and one part-time member of staff drawn from another department. I particularly enjoyed the developmental [aspects] of setting up a framework for a department and the day-to-day things like putting together schemes of work, revision exercises and assessing student performance.

After this experience, I took on the role of subject leader for history, combining it with social science, when one of my colleagues was on secondment. I had started my career in the history department. From there in 1988 I became head of humanities faculty, which incorporated geography as well as social sciences and history. In 1992 I became head of sixth form and the post of head of faculty passed on to a colleague. Under management reorganization between 1996 and 1997 the post of head of sixth form was changed to year leader for year 13, sort of Year manager. When my colleague who was head of history took early retirement, by default I eventually became subject leader for history again.

Contexts 2: National and institutional policy contexts
When we only had six or seven managers responsible for all the clusters [faculties] of academic subjects we used to reconcile a lot of differences in that group. The biggest thing was capitation [budget allocations] to faculties, and it was always a debate about how we were going to share it out … You could always predict who was going to come in with what [view] but at the end of each meeting we used to come up with some solutions. Even though there were winners and losers at least we talked about it. The fact that that faculty structure was dismantled on the advice of an OFSTED inspection in 1994/5 to get clearer lines of management was not strategically beneficial. The single site for decision-making was divided up among three curriculum managers working with 24 subject leaders. When we have meetings now the former coherence of decision-making has become fragmented. In a school this size there needs to be a filtering of ideas and perspectives before decisions can be taken coherently.

Constructing professional identity
What sort of leader?
I have always thought the priority is being a classroom teacher. To be a subject leader you should enjoy being a classroom teacher and should have a proven record as a classroom teacher. Not the most innovative but the most effective. You can show that to colleagues through the response of the students that you teach. I suppose at

this level we have to be judged by examination results as well at KS4. I have always seen my role within the department within which I have worked as taking a lead in terms of developing schemes of work, of monitoring standards, and discussing ideas within the team. Department colleagues see me very much as the ideas person in some ways, because I have enjoyed the examining work, the assessment, the curriculum development. I enjoy putting together teaching and learning packs. So I do the developmental work, they chip in with it and discuss it, and are then quite happy to implement it. Sometimes they will come to me to ask what we are to do next, and I say, well, we are on week 3 and we do this. Current members of my subject department have also got other responsibilities in the school. One is a year manager, so she is in a middle management post herself. And the other colleague is also a middle manager who is involved in higher education in the sixth form with myself.

Authority and influence:
What has made it different being a subject leader is being able to spread and pass on ideas on education to a larger group of people. I suppose within management structures at school, because you are part of a middle management team it enables you to share that knowledge within a group of other subject leaders or middle managers, as well as within your own department. I think the other thing about being a subject leader, even though that is your title, within your subject area you have to work as a team with your colleagues. I have always seen my role within the department within which I have worked as taking a lead in terms of developing schemes of work, of monitoring standards, and discussing ideas within the team. The team contribute to that rather than the leader being directive.

Culture, norms and values
What sort of relationships with colleagues?
We do share, I think, quite similar aims that we hope to build upon. We have had success, I think, quite consistent success at both KS4 and A level which has helped to build up our own confidence but I think sometimes we are still uncertain about our capabilities. We have grown up together as teachers. I have been in the post for 18 years, a colleague has been in post for 17 years, and the other teacher is approaching 10 years. I think we have always felt that we can improve. We have not thought that we have been in the job so long that we have nothing to learn. What I can rely on from them is that if there are any deadlines or any problems, any

issues about work, they will always keep me informed. So it is built upon teamwork, mutual trust and academic and professional respect.

We have this shared ethos that primarily we want to do the best for the students. We want to give them an appreciation of the subject. We want them to fulfil their potential. We want them to become critically aware and appreciate the subject even if they don't continue with it. What has given us a lot of satisfaction over the last three years is the increase in the numbers of students who have gone on from GCSE to A level. It has doubled. So we hope that we have helped students to make decisions and given them enjoyment and appreciation of what they have learnt.

Among ourselves if we experience any problems, personally or professionally, we will always step in for each other. I think we appreciate our strengths, as well as the limits to what we can do. I suppose we complement each other with personality as well. The department is the team that works together and shares ownership of that. As you grow older you can feel you only have to serve the next few years and are past your sell-by date, or, positively, you can take a department forward and make and develop new ideas and broaden the subjects that you teach.

What sort of vision for students?
You know we do not want to let the students down. I have always believed that there should be a certain joy from learning and an enthusiasm from learning. I appreciate that not everybody likes history and they do it because it is the most preferable of a number of options, none of which they really want to do. I feel that the skills that students develop through learning, even if they never do history beyond the age of 16, they have actually developed. I also believe that through education you can build up self-esteem. If you succeed at whatever level you are capable of, it will help to prepare you for whatever you go on to, into work, into further education, into your relationship to others. So learning is not just for the results, although of course people are pleased if they get good results, but it is the process of gaining knowledge and the personal and intellectual skills that go with that.

Morality of using power
We try to allocate resources on as fair a basis as possible. When we get the capitation for the department each year, I always protect some for development. Then I get from publishing companies one sample of any new publication and we look at the strengths of that book and its weaknesses. If my colleagues want that book I will try

to make sure that bids for that book get put through when ordering departmental resources. I won't go and order anything without their consultation.

We take decisions together as a department to fit the needs of groups of students. If one group of students doesn't get the resources one year, we will make sure they get them the next year. If we haven't got the money to buy an appropriate text we will work together to try to fill this gap by preparing our own resources using our own materials. I always discuss with my colleagues what groups there are to teach and try to allocate groups of students to staff as fairly as possible, I hope, within the constraints of timetabling and constraints of resourcing that we put into operation.

Projecting power and influence: acting in whose interests?

I sometimes have to do some bargaining with colleagues about the timetable when they have teaching hours to fill up and there are courses without teachers, using leadership/management strategies like, 'there are some gaps in the timetable, and there are some groups in vocational courses who are available or there is some non-exam RE', trying to draw them into something they may be good at. I know they don't want the vocational courses and I know, through experience, that they may not want to do non-exam RE, but I hope they can take the opportunity of choosing a subject to teach, with support and with discussion. But they make the decision.

[Observation of this middle leader at work with students suggested that his vision for their engagement with the subject was sustained through his positive interpersonal relationships with them and by his appeal to internal and external policy and social contexts in which they were working – e.g. school rules and macro-policy frameworks of National Curriculum and public examination board syllabuses and timetables – the demands of which it would be, at least implicitly, in their economic interests to meet.]

Struggles for self-fulfilment in particular organizational contexts

We now have a clerical assistant in the department who has been promoted to a senior administrative assistant and she is excellent. She was drawn from the main school office three years ago where she was just doing a clerical job. But she relates very well to students because her children are about a similar age. She has a wonderful personality and is very good at organizing. So I have tried to help and encourage her to build that role. Now we have hit an impasse. In terms of wage structure it is difficult to get her the remuneration she deserves, so we have put that matter in the hands of the governors. She also needs more office space so we are working towards turning a classroom in the area into an office with everything centralized. I got permission for this from the head at some point and have it on paper, so we are going ahead with it. If you feel something is important is going to benefit a wide range of colleagues and students then you go for it.

Whose vision was it anyway?

The foregoing raises as many questions as it resolves by making open to scrutiny the processes and complexities of decision-making without hiding them behind a jumble of rationalization or trying to force them into a functionalist framework that degrades the data through loss of interactionist and critical detail. Although this head of department consciously works within various contextual frameworks, which he acknowledges influence the way in which he and his colleagues work, his vision of his work as a leader derives from his personal and work-related history and the educational and social values he has acquired during his life.

However in whose interests he governs is debatable. The mask he wears to play his part (Hollis 1985) in school is at least two-faced, supporting colleagues but also supporting senior staff in implementing the institutional system, and this shapes his sense of professional identity. Gunter *et al.* (2001) comment on the contested nature of the place that middle leaders occupy in a school hierarchy. A third facet of this is a leader's own visions for what it means to be in a successful department or institution, to manage the same successfully, and to provide successful education to students. Forming part of that are her/his interpretations of what he/she thinks are staff colleagues' educational values and beliefs and what are the best interests of students in particular social, economic and political circumstances.

In this case the leader's vision for how the department ought to operate is clearly collaborative and, he would claim, is in the interests of his staff colleagues – they are busy middle leaders and teachers, too – to which they appear to assent by going along with his policies (Wolcott 1977). The overt hierarchical distinctions between him and his colleagues in managing the department makes it impossible to describe the sub-culture as collegial in any meaningful sense, and contradicts Hargreaves' (1994) notion of a genuine collegiality predicated on an absence of hierarchical relationships between members of a decision-making group or community. None the less, the collaborative sub-culture appeared to work successfully, according to all the members of the department who were interviewed.

He would claim he and his colleagues govern the department in the interests of the students, even those not interested in pursuing the subject to the next curriculum stage – and point to the increased numbers of students choosing to pursue the subject as evidence of this. But this evidence is weak since students' choices of subject will also be affected by the alternatives open to them. This subject might merely seem the best choice in a poor range of options, not really in their interests but allowing them to meet the organizational restraints on them to take a required number of subjects. Clearly he has a vision for the students, which reflects his educational values, and which he attempts to translate into a cultural framework within which he and his colleagues practise. But it is not clear how far they reflect the views and values of the students. So his construction of utopia is a teacherly one that makes certain assumptions about the needs and interests of the students rather than one that reflects the explicit views and values of the students for whom it is constructed.

The bottom line of his decision-making, however, seems to be that he and the department meet the requirements of the school system, for example, by 'persuading' staff colleagues to take lessons that they may not really want to teach. He is a conduit for the power of senior staff (Foucault 1977) so the interests of senior staff who have created particular organizational policies are served rather than those of any individual members of the school community, be they students or staff. However, at other times he is also a conduit for the needs of other staff, such as the clerical assistant, using his knowledge of school networks and decision-making to advance her cause.

His use of manipulation – 'using leadership/management strategies' – appears to fit with the views of Lenski (1986) and Hardy (1985) on how appeal to the rule frameworks of social systems is a less corrosive way of leaders maintaining control than direct coercion and confrontation. It allows leaders and followers to identify a common overwhelming coercive force (both of compulsion and reward), such as external social and policy contexts (e.g. passing particular public examinations), that allows them to assent to institutional policies and practices that sustain asymmetrical power relationships between members of the school community that they might not like and, in other circumstances, might challenge. It is when students, in particular, no longer perceive the force of those external policy contexts, perhaps because their chances of success in meeting such demands are very slight, that they begin to challenge the institutional demands made on them. The benefits of compliance no longer seem worth the loss of self-esteem associated with submission to socially constructed institutional and curriculum frameworks the purposes of which seem irrelevant to them.

In one sense this middle leader governs only to fulfil his interests and values. His vision for successful education guides his everyday practices, even if it cannot always be completely fulfilled. However, he would claim his values include taking account of the expressed needs of other people with whom he works, both staff and students, by listening to their voices and creating a culture of interdependency in which the assent of the governed, staff colleagues and students, is embedded. So perhaps he is governing in their interests too, at least within the constraints of the internal and external policy contexts of their work and those of the structures and processes of a hierarchical institution. Governing departments in secondary schools, or whole school institutions, need not be an autocracy forced coercively on unwilling subjects by appeal to external factors such as performance in school league tables, be they students or staff. It may not be democratic because of the asymmetrical power relationships in them but genuine consultation by leaders can allow other members of a community to influence decisions and gain some ownership of them.

5   The heart of the matter
The moral dilemmas of working in educational settings

Constructing work-related identities in schools

There is a dearth of humanistic enquiry on the professional lives and histories of leaders (Gunter and Ribbins 2002), especially middle leaders in schools. So this chapter explores how, like other teachers, leaders pursue the project of the self (Giddens 1991) through time, drawing on views and values they have developed historically in a variety of locations through their interactions with others in the workplace and beyond. In doing so it investigates how the histories of teachers holding formal post of responsibility in schools, such as middle leaders, affect the sub-cultures they construct in the departments for which they have been given responsibility. Emerging from this are the sources of the educational and social values that influence leaders' decisions – following the work of Ribbins (1997) – especially when guiding the construction of organizational cultures and subcultures and the perception of these enacted values by other members of the epistemic communities of their schools with whom they work most closely.

As with other teachers, leaders, at whatever level they work in the hierarchy of a school organization from classroom to senior staff board room, develop work-related identities through their interactions with other people, whether staff, students or parents, through time. Middle leaders, such as Key Stage coordinators, or heads of department, perceive themselves primarily as teachers rather than as managers (Busher 2002, 2005a). The terms 'leader' and 'manager' are used interchangeably here, taking the view that they are essentially two aspects of leadership, the former focusing on developing vision and purpose, the latter on the instrumentality of enacting practice. The term 'professional identity' is eschewed in favour of that of 'work-related identity' as the linked notions of profession, professionality and professionalism are strongly contested (Hoyle and John 1995) and do not add any extra clarity to the discussion about how teachers construct work-related identities to help them make sense of their working lives. Further it makes it difficult to talk about the construction by students and support staff of their work-related identities in school, since they are not usually classed as professionals yet clearly they construct identities for whatever milieu in which they find themselves, as several studies (e.g. Willis 1977; Benjamin 2002) have shown.

The development of the self is a reflexive project in which a person's development arises through their conscious and reflected-upon interactions with a range of other people (Giddens 1991) in a variety of settings, in which people constantly struggle with tensions between their espoused theories and their theories in action (Schon 1987) of what it means to be a particular type of actor in a particular community or organization. Benjamin (2002) points out how students carry out micro-cultural work to locate themselves in the different communities in and out of the school of which they have membership centrally or marginally. These communities include teachers (the formal authority system of a school), their class mates, their home community groups, their families. In constructing identities they try to create a persona that allows them to move relatively comfortably from one community to another without experiencing too much personal discomfort emotionally and socially or generating too much hostility from members of the different communities within which they locate themselves or are forcibly located by school organizational processes. In this argument, schools are construed as sites of policy processes (Grace 1995; Ball and Bowe 1992) that are sustained by asymmetrical and negotiable relationships of power between school members and stakeholders. In these institutions organizational structures are no more, though no less, than the historical outcomes of negotiative processes, the reflections of past and present hierarchical relationships within the school that are sustained and eroded by changing socio-political contexts.

The pursuit and enactment of self-identity by people is a central aspect of their development of agency (Giddens 1991). Greenfield (1993) perceives this process being made up of acts of individual will and practice, an existential view according to Ryan (2003). Giddens (1984) construes it as part of an interactive process in which people engage with other people to construct communities, social systems and structures. In school these other people include teachers, senior staff, students and their parents and carers, support staff and governors, as well as people peripheral to the school process. People's work-related identities are grounded in their individual histories, personalities and work-related experiences (Nias 1999; Goodson 1992; Thomas 1995), including, for staff in schools, their experiences as students in various institutions (e.g. Gersten 1995). It reflects in part phenomenological perspectives through which subjects try to make sense of the world by reflecting on their constructions of reality in the light of those perspectives presented by other people and by social structures in which they live and work.

Although interactions with other teachers form a central aspect of school leaders' work-related relationships and help to shape their identities as well as the cultures of their epistemic and pastoral communities (academic dempartments and year groups), so, too, do their interactions with students and their parents, and with support staff. Support staff (Busher and Blease 2000; Busher and Saran 2000) and students are important actors in the processes of schooling and have clear insights into what constitutes effective teaching and learning (Rudduck *et al.* 1996; Rudduck and Flutter 2000) and supportive environments for learning.

Students, too, develop work-related identities in schools. Starratt (1999) argues that learning is an active process rather than a consumerist one and that it is students, not teachers, who have 'the work of sense making, of producing knowledge suggested by the curriculum, of performing that knowledge in a variety of assessable products, of explaining how those performances and productions reveal their understanding' (p. 23). Benjamin (2002) points out that this might, like teachers, involve them in juggling multiple identities to cope with the variety of communities (or sub-communities) within school and outside it of which they have membership. Competing and overlapping membership of various communities faces people with tensions about how they present themselves – manifest certain values that allow them to gain and/or retain membership of communities – in such ways that they can retain a sense of integrity even if some of those different communities collide. Managing such multiple identities for students includes considering how they present themselves to other students of the same age group, as well as to older and younger students, in school; to teachers; to parents; to friends out of school. For teachers the overlapping sub-communities might be the different departments within that they work; their interest groups; their work groups in school and on fieldwork or in sport.

How creative people can be in such micro-cultural work depends on the extent to which the communities of which they have membership overlap and the range of roles available to them in the expectations of the other members of their communities if they are to remain respected and wanted members of those communities. As students, like other people, are unlikely to value equally all the sub-communities of which they have membership, especially as they get older they will develop persona that give them strongest membership of those communities that they value most highly, even if it leads to various forms of conflict with other communities of which they have membership. For example, some students may prefer to be accepted by and acceptable to their peers in the way in which they behave even if it leads them into conflict with teachers.

The development of the self is located in a variety of socio-political and economic contexts – discussed in Chapter 2 – that have considerable impact on the work of teachers and the achievements of students as learners. Students and staff use dialogic and reflexive ways to engage with and make sense of their experiences in these various contexts and to develop core educational and social values to guide their actions consciously and unconsciously (Hodgkinson 1991; Begley 1999a). The location of their work within these contexts and organizational frameworks leads teachers and students to build understandings of power and powerlessness into their identities, as Smyth *et al.* (2000) point out, as well as of the impact of contextual factors of race, gender (Osler and Vincent 2003), creed and socio-economic status. These contexts have important historical dimensions, as do people's biographies (Thomas 1995). The histories that people, be they students or teachers or support staff, have experienced since childhood act as contexts that shape their current educational values and beliefs and views on practice. It gives rise to the cultural capital they carry with them (Bourdieu and Passeron 1977), as is evident in some of the research on senior leaders (Ribbins 1997).

To people workers, such as staff and leaders at any level in schools, understanding people's actions in terms of how they are constructing their self-identities in particular contexts is essential to being able to work with them successfully. Some people use this knowledge immorally to exert power over people, to coerce them (Etzioni 1961), or to manipulate or manage them (Foucault 1977). Blase and Anderson (1995) suggest that leaders in schools use power in a variety of ways to shape the work of colleagues and students. The choices that individual leaders make about how to use their knowledge of students' and colleagues' developing work-related selves involve value-laden or moral decisions about how to act to create more or less harm and in whose interests. Teachers are sharply aware of this when working with students. Promoted post-holders in schools, too, have to be conscious of this when working with teachers and other staff as well as with students.

Developing work-related values

For leaders in schools, as for everyone else, reflection upon their lived experiences and their struggles with social and institutional structures gives rise to a bundle of personal, educational and social values and beliefs that they try to enact (Greenfield 1993). How they try to live out their values and beliefs reflects the personhoods they have developed (Aubrey *et al.* 2000) and this affects the quality of their relationships with people, be they students, teachers or other people with whom they have to work and live. Values lie at the core of how teachers build relationships with their colleagues and students. Hodgkinson (1991: 164) talked about educational leaders being in an area of ethical excitement. Leaders who want to build an emancipatory organizational culture that encourages collaborative learning or professional learning communities focus on encouraging staff and caring for students, encouraging dialogue, encouraging openness and risk-taking, and maintaining relationships while wrestling with ambiguity and professional disagreements.

Through their experiences as teachers and trainee teachers that are shaped by socially constructed discourses and stories of acceptable practice (Smyth *et al.* 2000), teachers and promoted post-holders develop a range of espoused theories (Schon 1987) about teaching and learning and about appropriate relationships with students, parents and colleagues. These reflect their attempts to synthesize their values and beliefs with the educational and social practices they are expected to enact by dominant people and discourses at national, local and institutional level in education. Many of these expected practices reflect qualities commonly associated with effective teaching and effective teachers (Wragg *et al.* 2000; Cooper and McIntyre 1996) in an anglophone western society. In attempting to integrate their values and those expected of them, people have to reflect on their work-related practices and the values that underpin them. In doing so they help to construct and reconstruct the cultures of the communities or organizations of which they have membership, and those of the formal and informal sub-communities, such as subject departments and interest groups, within those organizations to which they belong, since each is a nexus of values and attitudes that members have constructed to give themselves a sense of identity and purpose (Schein 1992).

The central importance of values led Begley (1999a) to consider that the first responsibility of leaders is to reflect on and make explicit their own values, then to consider other people's values and finally to engage in dialogue with other people to resolve values conflicts. MacBeath and MacDonald (2000) suggest that decision-making based on the use of moral authority grounded in shared professional and social values is most likely to promote the social cohesion and collegiality that can lead to improved practice. West *et al.* (2000) thought that leaders who want to sustain school improvement through building an emancipatory organizational culture while wrestling with ambiguity and work-related disagreements have to 'build up a consensus around high order values that members of the school community can relate to and believe in' (p. 40).

Ethical and transparent approaches to decision-making are more likely to be sustained by the values embedded in distributed leadership (Gronn 2000; Woods *et al.* 2003) than by leadership styles that are more autocratic or corporate in focus. The former involve fostering positive interpersonal relationships based on shared values between people to construct a sense of community (Sergiovanni 2001), and allowing leadership for particular aspects of joint activity to be shared among members of the group or community (Gronn 2002). In communities where there is trust between members, Smyth *et al.* (2000) argue that participants are likely to sustain a critical dialogue, whatever position they hold, about the practices of teaching and learning and the development of those to better meet the needs of all students. Gunter *et al.* (2001) translate this into teachers' practices in the classroom, discussing how teachers as leaders of learning in the classroom – meaning any site where formal learning is intended to take place – work successfully with students to construct learning processes that are meaningful and relevant to all of them and are based on agreed and negotiated values.

The more powerful people are, the more they are able to influence the values that become embedded in the communities of which they have membership. People's experiences of the use of power in and through communities of which they have membership deeply affects their sense of self and of agency. Ethical and moral discourses also offer explanations for why people prefer to resist some directions in which leaders want to take institutions, whether under pressure from external agencies or of their own volition, when those people find on principled grounds that the proposed directions conflict with their espoused work-related or personal values. Leaders try to sustain and transmit particular values that they have espoused but their ability to do so is constrained by the influence and authority to which they have access in institutions (Bennett 2001) and by the views and values held by colleagues (Lukes 1974). Murphy (1992) suggested that leaders who veer towards being creative and empowering might be 'servant leaders' or educative leaders (Duignan and McPherson 1992) who try to permit other peoples voices to be heard in decision-making to promote the interdependence and professional development of colleagues (Ribbins 1992) within the constraints of the internal organizational and extra-organizational policies and structures that exist.

The educational values that teachers hold or are expected to hold are a considerable source of tension for them. When the social and educational values they hold are in conflict with those values asserted in the external environment of schools, or of their subject departments, by powerful people or dominant discourses, especially when they are expected to accept these asserted values, teachers are likely to feel coerced (Etzioni 1961) or browbeaten (Allix 2000). As a consequence they are likely to feel unwilling to implement such values and their associated practices and therefore do so half-heartedly. Such values for education might come from members of the social and business communities that a school serves, or central government, or members of various ethnic and cultural minorities that a school serves. For example, the last may want to see elements of their cultural values included in the school curriculum, be that through particular dress codes of students, opportunities for particular forms of worship, use of heritage languages and customs as an integral part of the pattern of the school year and of school practices, or the use of culturally appropriate stories and examples in various aspects of the academic curriculum.

Some of the central educational values that teachers hold relate to their particular subject interests or to particular aspects of their work in school. For example, teachers of academic subjects are usually enthusiastic about at least some of the topics encompassed by their subject areas, although this might lead to conflict with other teachers when both want scarce resources for their work. Teachers might hold a variety of different pedagogical values about how teaching and learning should be carried out, some of which will be related to their subject epistemic communities into which discourses they have been inducted during their time studying a subject and their period of professional training. Other values are likely to be related to their perspectives about what are appropriate relationships between staff and students of different ages. Some values that teachers hold and try to enact will be related to their histories and social interests (their gender, ethnicity, family and faith backgrounds), while others will be related to the posts they hold in the formal organization of a school and the work-related experiences they have had of how people act in such posts in the course of their career. In one study (Busher 2002) it was clear that participants developed a range of educational and social values that formed the core of their work-related identities. These values covered many aspects of their work such as working with students, effective teaching, work cultures and the morality of managing departments or sub-communities.

Developing people's values and interests: the centrality of life history

Who people are, the personhoods they have developed (Aubrey *et al.* 2000; Giddens 1991), affects how they act in their formal and informal roles in their institutions. The views and values encountered early in people's lives and careers continue to influence their reflections and choice of enacted values in particular work situations when they are more established as teachers, leaders or support staff in schools. This choice is the outcome of an iterative process of comparing their historic social experiences with a framework of values that they have constructed in order to develop a coherent sense of self (Giddens 1991). In turn this is reflected in the cultures and sub-cultures of the schools and departments that leaders come to govern.

Participants in one small-scale study (Busher 2002) were deeply affected in their views on teaching and their values for education by their childhood experiences. A female middle leader described her father as 'like a walking encyclopaedia about the world'. This, and where she lived as a child encouraged her to become a geography teacher. Another middle leader was impressed by his uncle's lifestyle. 'He seemed to have a life in which his teaching was an important part, but also he could get away from the work.' It led him to choose teaching as a career rather than his family's usual business. Another male middle leader attributed some of his social values directly to his father. '[I try] to treat people as equally as possible and as fairly as possible. [My Dad] puts a lot of standing on justice and how you should treat other people.'

Teachers' positive memories of their time at school and university shaped their educational values. One female middle leader 'loved school because I did everything and I got into everything. It was more my whole school experience – being with other people, and doing stuff [than a particular subject].' They commended those teachers who 'really had a good knowledge and enthused about it' (female middle leader) and who gave students helpful and rapid feedback on their work because 'our books were always marked' (male middle leader), and who always made lessons 'an enjoyable experience for whichever pupils you happen to be teaching in whatever type of school' (male middle leader). They applauded teachers who they perceived to be kind and fair but also quite strict and gently aloof from their students. They appreciated those teachers who were 'willing to go the extra mile' (female middle leader) with them not only in helping them intellectually but also in taking the trouble to get to know them as people, acknowledging their personal and social developmental needs as well as their academic ones.

These memories included examples of what they said were successful teachers from their perspectives as students. One middle leader described a teacher who, he found, 'made learning so much easier and so much fun. [He] just seemed to know what he was talking about and he enthused about it. And that in turn made us want to learn about it more.' Another recalled fondly a particular model of participative leadership used by teachers conducting fieldwork. 'The teachers were part of your group. They talked to you in a nice way. If they asked you to do something they'd explain why they wanted you to do it. They would do it in a pleasant way. Everything was quite calm.' Both teachers said their experiences influenced the ways in which they now tried to teach.

Unpleasant experiences, however, also affected teachers' views of acceptable practice in teaching and they vowed not do the same in their lessons. One recalled how RE lessons were confined to copying and reading from the Bible. Another remembered being humiliated by a teacher in front of her class for a poor piece of work in RE. She remembered, 'Miss H saying "your disciples look like glamorous women". And they did. It was a very funny comment, actually, but not funny to me as a seven year old ... obviously I bear a grudge.' One male middle leader remembered how bullying by prefects had been an everyday experience when he had been at school and was determined it should not happen in his subject area.

Middle leaders' experiences in schools and other educational institutions led several teachers to consider that students' personal and social needs had to be acknowledged before they could be helped to learn successfully. Said one, 'You can't actually educate students, people, when they are unhappy or disturbed or there are things going on in their background.' It is noticeable that teachers' views of successful teaching, derived from the time when they were students, fit well with the canons of literature on effective teaching (Wragg *et al.* 2000; Cooper and McIntyre 1996), suggesting that students may be valuable sources of information on teaching and leadership for teachers and potentially important sources of data for evaluating teachers' and school practices.

Some teachers also indicated how experiences outside their schools and colleges as youngsters had affected their views on teaching and what they valued in teaching. One commented on her experiences doing outdoor pursuits, 'which I thought was fab. Geology [at university] involved a lot of field courses, a lot of working outside and doing things as a team.' Another found that she 'had a talent for relating to young children ... from inner city New York. I enjoyed that, the challenge ... disciplining them, being in charge, actually making sure that they did what they were supposed to do in the time they had to do it ... being responsible for them and for their welfare' and she valued 'the [positive] response that you got from these difficult kids'. Others commented on the influence of their experiences on the sports field or in the theatre on their choice of career and on their views on relationships between teachers and students.

As teachers entered the early stages of their careers their unfolding work-related identities were developed through a widening range of experiences which led one to discover that 'a lot of my skills lie in the classroom and in teaching, but a lot of my other skills lie in my organization, and my ability to get things to come together, and to be planned and to be thorough'. Others commented on the importance of sponsorship by more senior staff in their schools in helping them develop not only projects in school but to go on relevant courses and take a broad view of teaching and learning. One male middle leader said it helped him see 'how the school operated not just in relation to schools locally but nationally as well'. Lack of such support and working in poorly managed departments threatened to inhibit some participants' careers.

The social worlds that teachers inhabited outside work also influenced their careers and their work-related identities. Two teachers moved jobs for personal reasons – getting married, in one case, and the needs of his wife and children in another. Supportive social networks in school as well as shared educational values dissuaded one participant from changing jobs. As she explained, 'I like it here and I agree with a lot of the philosophy, although the school has had difficult times recently. And this is where I have put down my roots.'

Deconstructing educational leaders' educational values

Teachers' educational values are likely to focus on how teachers and students, and possibly teachers and parents, should interact to promote learning and sustain order. They may also include statements of appropriate relationships between people holding different formal positions in the hierarchy of a school community or organization. Once they are promoted to some formal leadership post in a school, their values are also likely to encompass statements about how to interact with staff colleagues holding non-promoted posts. Middle leaders in one study (Busher 2005a) indicated a range of work-related values that they held about:

- pupils/students
- effective teachers and teaching
- the value of their teaching subject
- preferred values for working in school departments
- managing staff in formal school teams
- allocating resources to students.

Values for students

Teachers perceived students as important actors in the process of constructing the school culture who should be happy in their work and enjoying their lessons; have a sense of achievement whatever assessment grades they gained; and have a sense that teachers cared for them so that they cared about their lessons, too. They wanted students to respect themselves and build up self-esteem by 'acknowledging students as individuals and then identifying those [strengths] and encouraging [them] to develop' (female middle leader). 'If you [a student] succeed at whatever level you are capable of, it will help to prepare you for whatever you go on to, into work, into further education, into your relationship to others' (male middle leader). To do this they 'thought it important to teach students social skills … as human beings through teaching trust and responsibility' (female middle leader) and treat their students equitably through providing differentiated 'schemes of work and worksheets … for the more able [students] to extend them/push them, and also for the less able … so the curriculum is accessible to all students' (female middle leader).

Values for effective teaching

Middle leaders perceived themselves first and foremost as part of a community of teachers, not separated from it by the management post they held. Not only did participants think it important for them to be seen to be effective classroom practitioners to gain the esteem of their colleagues, but so, too, did their colleagues. All of the middle leaders (Busher 2002) taught for at least two-thirds of the timetable, although they wished they taught less and complained that it made it difficult to fit in their other duties, especially their pastoral ones.

Their beliefs about effective teaching were manifested in a passionate enthusiasm for their subjects, which one described as 'teach in a dynamic way', in making learning enjoyable in their subject, and in helping students to achieve the best outcomes they could in their subject areas. The last included managing carefully the resources available in a department so they were accessible to as many students and teachers as possible. They took it for granted, but emphasized it, none the less, in the stories that they told, that all teachers should have a very good knowledge of their subject and be dynamic in their teaching of it. However, not all their colleagues shared their enthusiasm, one describing his (female) middle leader as 'too enthusiastic' and only interested in career advancement.

Middle leaders wanted to sustain and enhance their colleagues' and students' performances. These were linked to values that acknowledged those of the external framework of schooling: setting challenging standards of performance to all students in a subject area, linked to National Curriculum age-related levels of performance, and monitoring carefully the quality of their performance against those standards. Some of their colleagues did not entirely welcome 'doing performance management but recognize that it is a hoop that they have to jump through. I think it is quite a positive and productive thing. If you do it every so often it makes you think a little bit more about what you are doing. That has a knock-on effect on the rest of your teaching' (female middle leader).

Values for working in departments

Middle leaders emphasized their focus on teaching and learning, not managing, seeing their key values as meeting the learning needs of their students (Busher 2002). For them, management and leadership in all its manifestations was merely a means to that end. Their core values for achieving this were fairness, compassion and effectiveness, rather than competition and meritocracy. Observation of the middle leaders at work and the comments of their colleagues supported these emphases.

Middle leaders preferred to work collaboratively with their colleagues, rather than promoting an individualistic and competitive ethic, and encouraged department members to be friendly and supportive colleagues. They thought it a key aspect of their work to help generate such collaboration through discussing with their colleagues the schemes of work and means of monitoring student performance. Consultation with colleagues took place formally in department meetings and informally in corridors and staff rooms. In one department this happened formally. In one department the formal meetings took place 'every Thursday morning and a faculty meeting once every four or five weeks on a Monday afternoon after school'. However, the same male teacher asserted that the 'real running takes place constantly throughout the day, breaks, lunchtimes and during lessons. We are confident enough to wander into each other's lessons without fear of upsetting anyone. It is run very well. It does not need to be strict.'

Observation of middle leaders teaching and working with colleagues and participants' comments suggested that shared perspectives on educational issues linked to shared values helped teachers to operate as self-supporting communities rather than as autocratically directed teams (Busher 2002). The importance of the informal communications was illustrated in one case by their weakness. In one school, teachers whose classrooms were located physically away from a department complained about not always being so well consulted as those based in the subject area's suite of rooms, but agreed it was because of their location, not because of carelessness by the department's leader.

Middle leaders encouraged collaborative working by sharing intellectual resources with colleagues through developing schemes of work, offering ideas for developing a varied repertoire of teaching methods, or sharing their own craft knowledge on working with students and parents and organizing departments. In this they showed their expert knowledge as teachers, one of the values they considered important for middle leaders to possess. They also worked collaboratively with colleagues when taking decisions about developing the curriculum to meet pressures from external policy contexts, local community and civic contexts, or the policy directives of the school's senior management team.

Support for collaborative working was linked to values of developing social communities among their colleagues, the emphasis being on supporting each other personally as well as professionally when necessary. One teacher in a department commented that 'although we are so diverse, we chat in the staff room. At the end of term we have a faculty meal. Some of the faculty go to the pub on a Friday, not every week. Other members go at different times.' Other departments had social gatherings quietly over dinner occasionally at the end of a term.

The preference for collaborative working did not disguise the hierarchical power relationships that existed in departments between middle leaders and their colleagues, although there was acknowledgement by middle leaders of the collective power of departmental colleagues, too. Several middle leaders recognized that they had to gain the consent of their colleagues to policies and policy implementation if it was to work effectively. In some cases they indicated that this might lead to them modifying how a policy was implemented to take account of colleagues' views, even if a policy, whether theirs or that of senior staff, was implemented largely unmodified. As one middle leader explained, she was accountable for the work of the department to the school's senior management team, as well as perceiving herself as an advocate for her subject colleagues' views to the senior management team, perspectives her departmental colleagues endorsed. If necessary, she explained, she was willing to argue for her vision of her department against the views of her subject area colleagues, especially when it was lent support by the policy initiatives of the senior staff. Other middle leaders expressed similar senses of tension and contradiction.

Values for resource allocation

Middle leaders in the study (Busher 2002) claimed they allocated resources on a principled basis, supporting Simkins' (1997) view that resource allocation in schools is a value-laden activity. Resources were allocated to try to meet students' needs equitably within the budgetary frameworks available so that, as one middle leader explained, 'if one group of students doesn't get the resources one year, we will make sure it does the next year ... if there are gaps [in curriculum resourcing] we will work together to try to fill them by preparing our own resources using our own materials'. Another middle leader asserted that she and her colleagues tried 'to get resources that will benefit the pupils, [to] spend the money fairly and equally across all the pupils, [and] make sure all the pupils have the right texts and other materials'.

Part of the process of establishing equity in departments, middle leaders claimed, was establishing a strong central administration in their departments: 'central resources and common schemes of work, common assessment, common [student] records that we put on to Excel that can be monitored to see how different classes are doing and that staff are meeting deadlines' (female middle leader). Another middle leader complained at what he perceived as the selfishness of some colleagues who did not return textbooks and worksheets, among other resources, to the stock cupboard, making it difficult for teachers and other classes to access these. Some teachers concurred with this view, preferring a minor loss of freedom in complying with a bureaucratic system of stock control to ensure that people in the department had equitable access to resources for lessons. Some teachers ruefully acknowledged that such systems also monitored teacher practice but acknowledged the legitimacy of this accountability in the educational system in which they worked.

Discussion

Many of the values that middle leaders said underpinned their current practices, and were observed to be enacted through them, seemed to reflect
their experiences as young people and students themselves. This supports
the views of Giddens (1991) and Greenfield (Ryan 2003) that the construction of self-identity takes place around the development of a personal
values system and is a reflexive rather than merely a social replicative
process. It also lends support to Ribbins', (1997) view about the importance
of people's histories in the development of leaders' perspectives on their
work, and to the views of Thomas (1995) as well of those of Measor and
Sikes (1992) about the groundedness in history of the values and views that
people enact in their interpersonal interactions, whether at work or not. To
some extent it shows how people's personal and social contexts affect their
personal and work-related development.

Although teachers to some extent tried to replicate their own positive
experiences as students for their current students, none the less they
seemed to reflect on their positive and negative experiences of schooling, as
well as on their personal histories, to create a synthesized, coherent and
enacted system of values and practice for themselves as teachers. This supports the view of the development of work-related identity as a reflexive
process (Giddens 1991) through which people constantly struggle to make
sense of the tensions they are experiencing between their sense of agency,
the views and values of other people, and the demands and values of the
systems in which they work.

The wealth of memory that middle leaders offered about their histories
raises some interesting issues. One shows the importance of values as filters
that shape the processes of teaching, learning and decision-making. This
emphasises the view of Begley (1999a) that values and morality are at the
heart of decision-making, and of Ribbins (1999) that all value-laden decision-making is political since choices that are made also include choices
that are rejected and this will shape the allocation of resources among
various groups of people, be they students or teachers. The second was the
emphasis that teachers placed on values of equity and fairness when
running their departments and how closely this seemed to match their
childhood memories of fairness and justice – or unfairness and injustice –
in particular educational locations that had driven the development of
their personal and work-related value systems and identities.

The norms they appeared to want to enact for their departments seem
to fit well with notions of collaborative working put forward for effective
schools and departments by Stoll and Fink (1998) and Harris (1999) and for
school improvement by Hopkins (2001). They also fit well with notions of
learning communities, such as those put forward by Bottery (2003).

However, although many of the teachers' values focused on the personal, social and academic development of students, students were not viewed as part of these communities or departments. Yet teachers' core values and practices seemed to revolve around the quality of the learning experiences their students might gain through teaching and how these experiences could be fostered through the ways in which they worked with their colleagues. For these participants at least, the core of their work-related identity centred around being a teacher, whether or not they held a promoted post, not being a manager. However, the middle leaders acknowledged the responsibilities of their posts which, they argued, offered a vehicle to improve the quality of learning and teaching in their departments.

Embedded in these values were debates and discourses around the legitimate uses of power, whether of authority or influence, with, through and over colleagues (Blase and Anderson 1995). It is not possible to make sense of the construction of communities and sub-communities (schools and departments) without understanding how power flows in them through individuals and collectivities or groups of people (Lukes 1974; Foucault 1977). Educational and social values were contested because every member of the epistemic and pastoral communities had had different life experiences through which they had developed their personal and work-related values and identities, and considered these of greater importance than any that middle leaders or senior leaders attempted to impose. These contestations took place in an asymmetrical framework of power between people and between people and existing social and organizational structures and systems (Giddens 1984) that were sustained by the values and policies of senior leaders and external factors such as government policy frameworks.

6 Creating cultures
Facilitating engagement

Leaders and the construction of cultures

Cultures in societies, communities and organizations are constructed by their members and manifested in the symbolic, practical, linguistic and interpersonal interactions of their members and in the social structures that are constructed, upheld and modified by them. Sub-communities or sub-groups in an organization, such as departments in a school, have their own sub-cultures that, although reflecting many of the facets of the culture of the whole organization, also have their own particular foci and perspectives. Holliday (2005) distinguishes between sub-cultures and small cultures to indicate the autonomy of cultures that communities or groups construct, a point that is returned to later in this chapter. Hopkins (2001) perceives culture as underlying and surrounding all the actions that go on in schools. Sergiovanni (1992) perceives the shaping of culture as the key function of leadership. Schein (1992) describes organizational culture as the social glue that holds an organization together, or more accurately, that holds together the people in an organization (in schools, that of course means staff, students, governors and parents).

In this post-modern world, Harrison (1994) asserts, there is a need to have a critical ethical perspective on educational leadership and management rather than a narrowly economic one. Ethical issues are involved in every decision that is taken by leaders, be they teachers or school principals, as they struggle to meet the competing demands on them. Greenfield (1993) talks about the moral complexity that flows inevitably through administrative action and sees the central realities of educational administration being human values. Values, which are at the heart of the cultures that are constructed by communities or sub-communities (schools, departments, identifiable groups of students), lead to action in everyday life and in educational administration. So institutions like schools, which Sergiovanni (1994) considers as much communities as organizations, are built through processes of debate, dialogue and interaction between individuals and between individuals and collectivities, leading to the implementation of some values and perspectives rather than others.

At the core of this is how leaders at all levels in schools work with other members of a school – teaching staff, support staff, students, parents and governors – as well as those stakeholders outside school who have an interest in its work, such as leaders of other local schools, LA officers and members of the local business and civic communities. This is reflected in the eight guidelines for action that Fullan and Hargreaves (1992: 112) offer for leaders in schools:

1. Understand the culture.
2. Value your teachers: promote their professional growth (find something you can value and praise in each teacher's work).
3. Extend what you value (breadth of vision that is inclusive of all good practice, not just including a leader's preferences).
4. Express what you value (remember the importance of using symbols to reflect values).
5. Promote collaboration, not co-optation (head teachers do not have a monopoly of wisdom, therefore vision building is a two-way process with staff, students and parents).
6. Make menus, not mandates (offer a choice of ways in which people can engage with teaching, learning and management successfully).
7. Use bureaucratic means to facilitate, not constrain, people's actions.
8. Connect with the wider environment.

The emphasis in establishing an appropriate culture that is likely to lead to effective learning in schools is on understanding staff as individuals; understanding how teachers perceive themselves as professionals – 'most teachers consider students' needs as paramount, even when these may be different from their own as employees' (Hall 1997: 152); on understanding the sub-cultures of particular subject areas; on understanding the focus of staff development in learning organizations; and on understanding students as individuals and how they perceive the processes of schooling (Rudduck and Flutter 2000), a view that has recently been enshrined in government policy in England (DfES 2004). There is also a need to recognize parents' views and to work more closely with them to sustain successful learning by students (Vincent 2000).

Understanding organizational cultures

The culture of an organization provides a means through which its members create and sustain meanings of it (Levinson *et al.* 1996). The culture provides a series of rules and guidelines through which its members can address problems they face (Trompenaars and Woolliams 2003). As cultures are social structures (Giddens 1984) that reflect the socially constructed beliefs and values of the members of the collectivities, they are likely to change through time through the interactions of the members of the collectivities with each other and with the socio-political contexts in which they are embedded (Schein 1992). The beliefs and values of a culture are manifested in various ways through rituals, ceremonies, rules, patterns of action and language which in a school are related to the curriculum and to its social organization (Beare *et al.* 1989). It helps members and outsiders to sustain particular identities (Schein 1992), recognizes the boundaries of particular social and institutional entities, and drives shared patterns of behaviour (Robbins 2003). As Hannerz (1992: 3) explained, 'culture is in some way collective' and 'underpins organizational structures, processes and practices' (Dimmock and Walker 1998: 385).

The culture of a school represents a nexus of particular values and beliefs and is sometimes described as its 'ethos' or 'atmosphere'. It focuses on what is constructed collectively by members of a group or institution, although some members of that group will be more influential in constructing it than others, as is discussed later. Sometimes the term 'climate' is used interchangeably with that of culture although strictly the former term, drawn from social psychology, focuses on describing people's perceptions of the interactions of one person with many, e.g. of a senior leader with her/his colleagues. One of the reasons for the complexity of understandings of what constitutes organizational culture is the ontology of the notion. As Schein (1990: 109) points out, 'culture lies at the intersection of several social sciences and reflects some of the influences of each, specifically, those of anthropology, sociology, social psychology, and organizational behaviour'.

Organizational cultures reflect to varying extents the dominant macroculture of the society in which they are embedded as well as the cultures of other social groups in their localities. Hofstede (1991) argued that attributes embedded in national cultures shape the expectations of behaviour inside organizations in a country so that there is a homogeneity of interpersonal relationships in both national and institutional arenas. One of the key elements of this, he argued, was how people respond to uncertainty and their expectations of leaders in uncertain times. Hopkins (2001) conceives a school's culture as a key element that filters the impact of views, values and policies in the external environment of schools and affects the implementation of new practices in teaching and learning at whole-school and classroom level. Below the level of a school's organizational culture are the sub-cultures of the academic or pastoral departments or organizational sub-units, such as a Key Stage area. This linkage of macro-cultures to individuals as mediated by organizational cultures and sub-cultures is shown in Figure 6.1.

The culture of a community or organization offers a framework of norms enshrined in rules, language, ceremonies and rituals that help members of that community to try to sustain its existing identity by expecting its members to act in certain ways in particular situations. So cultures become important means by which societies and communities reproduce themselves (Bourdieu 1990; Bourdieu and Passeron 1977). In particular they

Figure 6.1 The relationship of a school's culture and sub-cultures to the cultures in its external environment

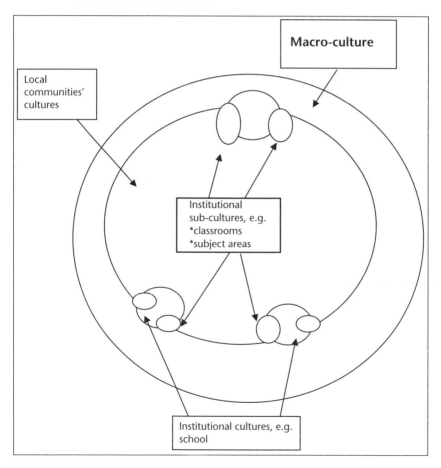

become important means whereby powerful people or ruling elites in those communities or organizations are able to sustain and reproduce those values and beliefs they hold important by expecting other members of those collectivities to act in such ways as to sustain those values and beliefs. Cultures, then, are conduits of power (Foucault 1977) for those people and groups who are already powerful. However, if senior leaders' values and power shape a school's culture considerably, so too do other social factors such as the national and local discourses around education, social relationships, gender, ethnicity and the socio-economic status of the members of a school, as well as a school's histories and the socio-political contexts in which it is situated (Busher and Barker 2003). Staff and students conduct their daily activities based on the values derived from their own national and community cultures and socialization (Hofstede 1991; Bourdieu *et al.* 1994) which provides a lens through which they interpret things and decide what is important.

Some organizations are said to have strong cultures with clearly defined norms of behaviour with which most members feel they have to comply as a result of their socialization into the organization through a system of rites, rituals and patterns of communication which make clear to members the patterns of behaviour and core values they are expected by powerful senior staff to exhibit when at work (Sergiovanni 1992, 2001). Other organizations have weak cultures that allow individuals and groups within them to behave with considerable autonomy, even when that action is in conflict with that of other groups or people in an organization. Deal (1988) argued that strong cultures were likely to be coincident with organizational success as they help people to work together successfully, while Reynolds (1998) argued that fragmented cultures tended to be associated with ineffective schools (see Figure 6.2, page 87).

Recent evidence from work by Kazmi and Hallan (2005) in schools with many ethnic minority children and James *et al.* (2006) in primary schools in socially disadvantaged areas of Wales suggests that school cultures that encourage successful learning are those which are strong, coherent and inclusive and subsume creatively cultural diversity rather than rigid monocultural perspectives. As social and cultural diversity increases in the population that a school serves, equity for students becomes a greater social priority for school leaders, requiring them to look not only at the internal processes of their schools but also at their schools' relationships with people in the local communities that they serve. It is only in this way that school disaffection can be tackled effectively (Riley and Rustique-Forrester 2002). Such diversity places school leaders in a quandary when what appears to be an equitable solution to a problem, for example the choice of a dress code for students, for members of one community that a school serves, may seem prejudicial to the interests of another. Determining how to balance and pursue alternative value-laden paths for efficiency, equity, effec

Figure 6.2 Cultures of ineffective schools

- The widespread belief that change is for other people.
- The belief among staff that the school should stick to its past methods of operation.
- The reluctance of individual staff to stand out from the prevailing group culture.
- The reluctance of many staff to attempt new things, fearing that they may fail.
- The blaming of factors external to the school by the staff for the failure of the school.
- The absence of any understanding among the majority of the staff about possible alternative policies.
- The belief among the staff that outsiders have little to contribute to turning the school around.
- The presence of numerous personality clashes, feuds and cliques within the staff group, in a setting of a generally grossly dysfunctional relationship.
- The unwillingness or inability of staff in the school to see that its 'presenting' problems of failure mask the 'real' problems of the institution.

(source: Reynolds 1998)

tiveness, excellence (Stout *et al.* 1994) and the personal growth and development of staff and students is a moral quagmire for school leaders at every level from Principal to classroom teacher.

It follows from this that organizational and community cultures and sub-cultures not only support change but can also provide considerable barriers to change if members of the communities expected to alter their working lives and practices feel their preferred values for practice to be under threat (Smith 2003). Individuals live in tension with the cultural frameworks of their civil societies and institutions because their personal values systems are only partially formed by these entities and only partially congruent with them. They also survive in asymmetrical power relationships (Giddens 1984) with these entities, being relatively powerless as individuals (Foucault 1977) but able to exert influence when they work together in coalitions or interest groups.

Leaders of educational institutions and their sub-units (departments or classrooms) have to work within the framework of the national macro-culture, as well as the cultures of local communities that surround a school (McMahon 2001). So the decisions and actions leaders take, whether to try to modify a school's culture or that of a sub-group in it, or develop a new policy, have to take cognizance of the expectations that people hold arising from their membership of communities external to a school as well as their membership of different sub-groups in it if the development is to be acceptable to other members of a school. Alvesson (1993) points out that although leaders are able to modify culture, they are also a product of it and constrained by it. In this discussion there is no suggestion that cultures and sub-cultures are fixed: rather that they are fluid, forever changing as people move in and out of organizations and the formal and informal groups within them, and as change occurs in response to internal and external pressures on an educational organization, as McMahon (2001) recognizes.

As the foregoing argument implies, within each organization and organizational culture there are likely to be a series of sub-cultures that are constructed by various groups within it, whether part of the formal structures of an organization, such as an academic department, or part of its informal processes. McMahon (2001) argues that organizational cultures are unlikely to be homogeneous and that groups and individuals in them will draw on and develop a variety of different, if related, culturally constructed perceptions of work in schools. The greater the number of such sub-cultures in a school, she argues, the more difficult it will be to bring about coherent change in a school. Foucault (1977) argues that culture is woven in and around organizational processes and structures. Sub-cultures play an important role in representing a sense of group identity, personal commitment and ways of doing things that help members of different departments to work closely together but also explain the sense of difference between departments. For example, different academic departments have different culturally defined methods for conducting enquiries or teaching their subjects and a set of conventions and modes of discourse for presenting results (Hodson and Hodson 1998).

In this discussion there is no suggestion that cultures or sub-cultures form part of what Hoyle (1986) perceived as the dark side of organizations or what Holliday (2005) described as the hidden counter-cultures of institutions and which Mullins (1996: 715) argued were often 'undiscussed and outside management control'. Here it is argued that people and collectivities, be they adults or students, in schools hold various sets of values and beliefs which interact with each other in the everyday workings of an institution. These reflect people's different views about what they consider to be important in their working, social and personal lives and they use what access to power they can gain to try to implement them. Leaders need to be keenly aware of this variety of legitimately held perspectives when trying to construct organizational cultures, especially inclusive ones that foster learning, since they represent the voices of people's personal and work-related identities that may offer a creatively different view of organizational development than the one propounded by powerful people in a school or department.

While the notion of a sub-culture might be suitable for groups of people working in formally constructed sub-units of an organization, it is more difficult to apply the notion to informal groupings of students, staff and parents in a school which are not located in the formal organizational structure of a school but, none the less, have a recognizable identity as a community or group within the community of a school. An alternative view of these group cultures, which avoids the implication that they are constructed as part of a hierarchy of cultures that diverge a little from the main organizational culture but are essentially part of it, is that of Holliday. He argues that these 'sub-cultures' are small cultures (Holliday 2004, 2005) within which are three main spheres of action: psycho-cultural features such as tacit protocols governing classroom interaction and relationships between staff and between staff and students; micro-political processes; and rubrics for maintaining order informally (Holliday 1994). In this view cultures of people (staff or students) are constructed by them as a means of coming to terms with dominant discourses of organizational or macro culture while retaining some of their own preferred values and beliefs. These cultures are not so much derivative from an organization's culture as constructions that combine elements from both the organizational culture in which they are immersed and their own values and beliefs. Such cultures allow people to continue to pursue what they think is important to them in life as well as meeting the demands of the institution in which they work or are compelled as students to attend. In other words these small cultures remain in the ownership and construction of those agents. As such they exist in the overlapping spaces of national macro-cultures, organizational cultures and local community cultures – large cultures, as Holliday (1994) calls them – and people's own personally developed values and beliefs.

The site and process of construction of these small cultures can be understood as one of hybridity (Bhabha 1994) which draws on elements from different dominant and marginalized cultural discourses to construct a new emergent set of cultural norms to guide practice for the members of the small culture that generate new identities. These could be work-related practices and identities among staff and students who are members of a new group. Examples of such groups are a new class at the start of a new school year, or a new department that is created as a result of organizational reconstruction.

Small cultures are a means of people finding a way not only to colonize dominant discourses, be those asserted organizational cultures or subject epistemologies and pedagogies, but of constructing their meanings for living and making sense of working in organizations. They can be linked to formal groups in schools, such as departments, or to informal groups among staff, students and parents. Only where they are linked to specific elements in a school's organizational structure might they be said to be equivalent to a sub-culture. For whereas the latter term emphasizes an orga-nizational perspective, the former emphasizes a personal one making the latter, perhaps, more appropriate for formal sub-units in an organization and the former more appropriate to informal groups of people. Both per-spectives challenge leaders to find ways of creating space for people to grow rather than merely asserting control over them.

An implication of the above is that within any school, people, be they staff or students, are likely to be part of more than one sub-culture or small culture as they are likely to be members of more than one group in the formal and informal processes of an institution. This is likely to involve them in some complex micro-cultural work of how to present themselves, especially if the sub-cultures of the different groups of which they have membership contradict each other in certain ways. For example, in staff rooms these sub-groups are sometimes manifested visibly in where people choose to sit or with whom to have beverages, such as is shown in Figure 6.3.

Figure 6.3 Looking in staff rooms

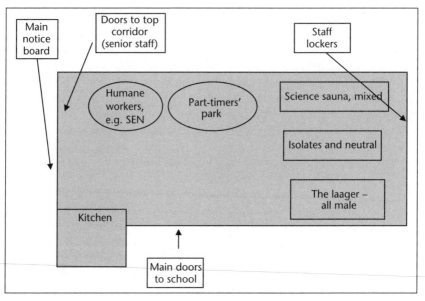

The importance of organizational culture

Organizational culture provides the social glue that helps hold an organization together (Robbins 2003) by making clear to members what they should say and do in particular circumstances, as is shown in Figure 6.4. It applies equally to senior staff as it does to others, but whereas senior staff are often sufficiently powerful to reframe the cultural rules – and sometimes simply ignore them – if they do not like them, other members of a school rarely have much access to manipulating what Giddens (1984) describes as social structures. Organizational culture is manifested in the way people interact, the implicit rules of the game, habits of thinking and shared meanings, symbols and metaphors (Schein 1992). Leaders who help to establish such rules use their access to power to frame them in such ways that they help to sustain their vision of the organization, or of the department or classroom. They are likely to expect other people, be they staff or students, to conform in their activities to the rules and practices laid down either implicitly in conventions or explicitly in codes of practice.

Figure 6.4 Functions of organizational culture

- Culture gives meaning to human endeavour.
- Culture generates shared values, beliefs and assumptions.
- Culture serves as a sense-making device that can guide and shape behaviour.
- Culture is socially shared and transmitted knowledge of what is and what ought to be.
- Culture ensures consistency of action among members of a group.
- Culture conveys a sense of identity for organizational members.
- Culture serves as a social glue that holds the organization together.
- Culture provides a common purpose for members by specifying the goals and values towards which an organization should be directed.

(source: Schein 1992)

Identifying clues that provide meaning in organizations places people in a better position to identify the cultural precepts that operate in a school or department. It allows people to understand what actions, be they physical, academic or in speech, and what rhetoric of values and beliefs are likely to gain acceptance, praise, rewards, recognition and, in some cases, security of work. Through these means communities and the more power-ful members of them are able to project their own preferred values and beliefs. The culture of an organization or sub-culture of a department is usually manifested through devices such as the following:

- the symbols and rituals they use
- the customs they adopt
- the myths and beliefs they adopt
- the images of school or department they adopt
- the language they use to talk about particular events or people
- the styles of communication they prefer to use
- the people and actions that they celebrate/denigrate as lived examples of their values
- the stories people tell of success or failure or 'normality'
- the explicit rules that govern how they behave/respond to other people
- the implicit norms that govern how they behave/respond to other people
- the goals they adopt
- the characters people choose to play in organizational groups.

Beare *et al.* (1989) suggest that these cultural attributes might be visible in the behavioural manifestations of people – rituals, ceremonies, rules, how teaching and learning is carried out; conceptual manifestations and metaphors – curriculum, language used, organizational aims and stories; and physical manifestations – facilities, uniforms, crests and mottos. Figure 6.5 (page 93) gives some examples of what cultural clues people might see in schools. Prosser (1999) points out the importance of visual ethnography as a means of identifying and making sense of such cultural artefacts in a school, as well as of the pitfalls of trying to interpret them.

A school's culture is manifested through the relationships that are encouraged between students and teachers, as well as between students, by particular approaches to teaching and learning. Ghosn (1998) suggested that teaching needs to focus on particular skills of 'listening, critical thinking, cooperation, conflict resolution, and problem solving' (p. 68) if teachers want to promote social justice and inclusivity. How people speak and act portrays and projects their value systems.

How time is used by leaders, be it in the timetabling of lessons or the sequencing of activities within a lesson, be it in timetabling meetings or scheduling social activities, projects values to other participants. Giddens (1984) discusses how control of time by some people imposes values on others. Lafleur (1999) points out that the designation of time for certain activities disempowers people from engaging in other activities. For example, students are expected to attend lessons, or give an explanation for non-attendance. To overturn such designations of time is an assertion not only of a person's authority – they are allowed to do that – and the diminution of the authority of the person from whom control has been taken away by asserting a hierarchy of power in the organization, but also of the importance (privileged value) of the reason for acting in that way. So when leaders in schools take students out of other teachers' lessons to arrange detentions with them for previous mis-demeanours, they are asserting the importance of moral behaviour by students, i.e. of compliance with the school's norms and codes of practice, as well as the power of the leader.

Another indicator of the culture of a school or department is the use of space and the layout of that space (e.g. the arrangement of classroom furniture, or the allocation of rooms to particular staff or subject areas). For example, in one department of a school, teachers move comfortably in and out of each other's rooms during lessons, not only to get resources but also to speak with each other without disturbing the lesson in progress. The same department shares a resource room, which all teachers use when necessary. The head of department does not have a separate office, although she does have her own teaching room, like all the other teachers in her department. This easy collaboration portrays a value of departmental cohesion, of which teachers in the department whose rooms are located outside the department suite feel they were less of a part. This use of space also

Figure 6.5 Developing a research agenda for mapping school cultures

Customs and conventions: 'how we do things round here'

- What are the formal and informal rules?
- Who are signalled as powerful people, who as the marginalized?
- How is that signalling done?
- What values are shown to be most/least important?

Beliefs

e.g. what beliefs do school staff hold about:
- pupils; pupils' needs; pupils' learning
- pupil grouping for teaching by age, sex and ability
- self-identity as a teacher/technician/secretary, etc.
- other people/colleagues, and how do they know?
- the purposes of (their) schools.

How do people weigh competing beliefs:
- e.g. need for academic excellence/needs of a subject *v.* needs for social inclusivity
- e.g. pupils' different learning needs *v.* an entitlement curriculum.

How do these beliefs affect the way in which teachers treat pupils and other adults?

What stories do people tell about success and failure?

Rituals and symbols (signal how dominant participants in social situations think those situations should be interpreted)

e.g. how are pupils seated in rooms/listed in registers?
- Whose work gets displayed in school/classroom or mentioned in Assembly?
- How are resources allocated to different pupil groups – and what is the impact on those groups that are given low priority in the allocation of resources?
- How are parents welcomed/involved in school processes?
Signalling the marginal: which students use non-specialist rooms; or are withdrawn from normal classes?

What impact does this have on pupils' self-esteem and self-identity?

Language (what language is used by people conveys values and perceptions including people's views of other people and the worth in which they hold them)

Creating a lexicon to gauge the culture – how do people talk about:
- other staff, e.g. site staff, clerical staff, senior management
- students, e.g. able students, students with recognizable learning difficulties?

What labelling do people use and does it facilitate or denigrate inclusion?

facilitates informal discussion and decision-making by staff that comple-
ments the formal processes of departmental meetings that occur each
month. Making sense of the uses of space by people, in part to indicate their
social groups or communities, can also be seen in playgrounds and staff
rooms, as Figure. 6.3 shows.

To cope with the tensions and the potential social conflicts that occur
in school communities, leaders need to listen to participants' voices, those
of students, staff, parents and school governors in particular, recognize
their interests and needs, and allow them to influence the curriculum and
organizational decisions that are made. The importance of students as internal actors in the construction of a school and of schooling (Day *et al.* 2000;
Ruddock and Flutter 2000), and recent central government policy encouraging the development of school councils, points to a re-emerging awareness of the importance of encouraging students to take a responsible part in
the government of their schools, an awareness that was largely extin-
guished in the 1980s and 1990s. School students have considerable impact
on the construction of its culture (Marsh 1997; Busher and Barker 2003),
whether or not they are commonly included in discourses about work-
related interactions in schools and whether or not they are conventionally
marginalized from discourses about school organizational process. Linstead
(1993: 59) describes this as students helping to write the texts of schools,
perceiving the construction of organizations as an intertextual process that
takes place between the authors and actors of it and in it. It raises questions
about how students' acute awareness of the processes of schooling and the
many insights they have of them (Rudduck *et al.* 1996; Rudduck and Flutter
2000; Flutter and Rudduck 2004) can be heard and acknowledged by staff
at all levels in order to contribute positively to the development of a school.

Another category of people in schools whose voice is often marginalized is that of students' parents. Work by Vincent (2000) among others has
underscored the importance of teachers working in partnership with
parents to help develop the successful education of students. In a study by
Osler *et al.* (2000) it became quite clear that schools that were able to deal
successfully with all their students were those that worked closely with
their students' parents and carers to help them understand what was
involved in schooling and how they could help their children to learn.
Such schools were also careful to reflect the heritage cultures of those
parents in the organization of the school and, where possible, in its academic curriculum. The impact of parents on a school is clearly illustrated in
Chapter 2.

Creating 'good' cultures to promote engaging schooling

Concept and problems

The first part of this chapter has discussed in general terms understandings of culture in organizations, its importance, and how it might be mapped or researched. This next part considers what might be the attributes of particular cultures in schools that might be said to foster the engagement of all students (and staff) with learning. It is argued that this is composed of two main parts, that of constructing a culture that focuses on developing teaching and learning so that the curriculum is accessible to all students in a school, and that of facilitating the inclusion of all students and their parents and carers in a school. It draws on a notion of utopianism (Halpin 2003) to suggest that what is constructed in these schema for success are as much wish-dreams that people try to work towards as statements of what is actually happening in schools, not least because the applicability of these schema in any school will vary with the quality of practice of the different formal sub-sections or communities of the school. It is as possible to have unsuccessful departments in schools that are generally well managed as it is to have effective departments in schools that are generally poorly managed.

The development of engaging schools takes place in particular socio-political and economic contexts which influence the ways in which schools are permitted to develop by central government in England at present and influence the development of cultures in those schools. Recent legislation points to an agenda of inclusion, for example the Education Acts of 2002 and 2004, the latter focused on a policy of 'Every Child Matters', the former on the importance of developing citizenship with all children in schools. There is a model for improving teaching and learning in schools, often referred to as school improvement, which is sustained by central government through its Standards Unit for education as well as through the Department for Education and Skills, which is shown in Figure 6.6.

However, some of the thrust of national policy is contradictory to this. For example, extending the choice of schools available to parents for their children through specialist colleges and academies only gives more choice to those who can take advantage of it, or who live in areas where realistic choice of schools exists. At present there is no firm evidence that such schools raise standards of teaching and learning. The National Curriculum is arguably exclusionary for some students, especially those with learning difficulties (Benjamin 2002), and fails to make adequate use of examples from the variety of cultural heritages extant in England in the early twenty-first century to make people from those heritage groups feel that their societal cultures are valued. Inclusion for children and their parents in school

Figure 6.6 Current school improvement programmes have many features in
common

- Changes in the processes of schools are now measured against their impact on pupil outcomes.
- The learning level and the instructional behaviour of teachers have been increasingly targeted for explicit attention.
- There is much greater emphasis on collaborative patterns of staff development that allow staff, through accessing knowledge of 'best practice' and research findings, to enquire more successfully into their own practice.
- There is much greater emphasis on encouraging schools to disseminate good practice and to network with other schools and teachers for help with their own practice.
- Auditing existing school and classroom processes and comparing these with desired end state is carried out using qualitative and quantitative data.
- There is increased emphasis on organizationally well-structured programmes of improvement so that all staff engaged in it are involved equitably.
- There has been a much greater appreciation of cultural change in order to embed and sustain school improvement.

Which are linked to various school improvement strategies:
- a commitment to staff development
- practical efforts to involve staff, students and the community in school policies and decisions
- transformational leadership approaches
- effective coordination strategies
- serious attention to the potential benefits of enquiry and reflection
- a commitment to collaborative planning activity.

(source: Hopkins and Reynolds 2001: 462–3, 469)

seems to be at a price of conformity to particular socially derived norms of behaviour that are put forward with the support of central government, limiting the flexibility with which teachers can respond to the local needs of students in their communities.

There is a shortage of joined-up practice between schools and other social agencies generally in England and Wales, particularly for certain groups of children: looked-after; traveller; refugee and displaced children, where social problems are a major cause of problems that students may have with schooling (Osler *et al.* 2000). Benjamin (2002) noted that underlying causes of student exclusion relate strongly to conflicts between students' social backgrounds (and the micro-cultural work they do to position themselves in their communities) and the social expectations of staff in their schools. In the main this leads to a considerable amount of official and unofficial exclusion of students from schools as students struggle to cope with the difficult socio-economic and emotional circumstances in which they sometimes find themselves and schools struggle to cope with them. In addition to official fixed-term and permanent exclusions, Osler *et al.* (2000) found numerous examples of unofficial exclusions or unspecified absences, which some head teachers justified as creating a cooling-off period for the students while alerting the parents that there was a behaviour problem.

These exclusionary cultures are constructed by people reacting to a variety of events linked to student behaviour but often these are trigger events ('headline reasons'), not the underlying causes. They reflect what dominant social discourses describe as unacceptable behaviour, illustrating Foucault's view (1977) of how notions of criminality are socially constructed at particular points in time. In one LA, Osler *et al.* (2000) found these trigger events to be as follows:

> Verbal abuse on staff (26.8%); physical attack on staff (6.8%); verbal abuse to other students (7.1%); physical attack on other students (23.1%); indecent behaviour (1.5%); damage to property (6.2%); abuse of alcohol (0.4%); abuse of drugs (1.9%); abuse of solvents (0.3%); tobacco smoking (3.5%); theft (2.4%); other reasons (19.4%).

The proportions of exclusions caused by particular events are shown in parentheses. In one urban LA an education officer suggested that physical aggression, much more than drugs, was a common reason for exclusion. Indecent behaviour, usually by boys to girls, was an occasional cause. Arson was also cited as a major cause, but this covered everything from starting a major fire to a child being seen playing with matches.

The real causes of exclusion, explained several education officers in the study by Osler *et al.* (2000), were the various social factors that underlay student misbehaviour and were rarely addressed adequately. These included students in homes suffering family crises or disturbed social circumstances; students who were former refugees; students who lacked sufficient command of English to access the curriculum adequately; students who moved frequently between schools (*TES*, 4 June 2004: 4). A particular example of the last was students who were looked after by local authority social services. In being transferred from one foster home to another their schooling was often disrupted, and if they were in a local authority home it was sometimes difficult for a school to know whom to contact about a particular student's academic achievement or social behaviour (*TES*, 4 June 2004: 4). Gender and race were two further relevant underlying factors. Boys were more likely to be excluded than girls: ten times more likely in primary schools and four times more likely in secondary schools. African-Caribbean boys were generally over-represented in the numbers of students excluded in proportion to their numbers in the school population, but in some urban communities other ethnic minority male students, notably those of

Pakistani origin, were also over-represented (Kazmi and Hallan 2005).

Developing cultures of inclusion

Developing cultures in schools that foster positive interpersonal relation-ships based on shared values between people working together helps to construct a sense of community (Sergiovanni 1992, 2001). This is most likely to sustain a critical dialogue about the practices of teaching and learn-ing and the development of those to better meet the needs of all students (Smyth *et al.* 2000). Hopkins (2001) suggests that particular collegial cul-tures are most likely to promote improvements in teaching and learning, at least in a western anglophone society.

Such cultures are likely to have the characteristics of those of improv-ing schools claimed by Stoll and Fink (1998) – see Table 6.1 – which also seem to reflect the characteristics of effective schools and departments (Sammons and Mortimore 1997). This points to synergies between success-ful learning communities and high achievement, not to a conflict between the two. At the core of both lies the nurturing of others to promote learn-ing, which has been put forward as one of the main purposes of schooling (Cooper *et al.* 2000), especially in primary schools (Nias 1999).

Table 6.1 Norms of improving schools

Attributes	Examples from teacher talk
Shared goals	We know where we are going
Responsibility for success	We must succeed
Collegiality is welcomed	We are working together on this
Continuous improvement	We can get better
Lifelong learning	Learning is for everyone
Risk taking is acceptable	We learn by trying something new
Support is acknowledged	There is always someone there to help
Mutual respect	Everyone has something to offer
Openness	We can discuss our differences calmly
Celebration and humour	We feel good about ourselves

(source: Stoll and Fink 1998)

Moving towards a more inclusive culture within a school takes time. The policies most likely to support inclusion are those that are develop-mental, reflect current circumstances of the school, set realistic goals for the future and are constructed around strategic steps for getting from one position to the next. One of the principal tools for this is the school devel-opment plan which needs to contain policies for reducing exclusions, developing equal opportunities, especially for children with special educa-tional needs, promoting staff development and strengthening links with parents (Osler *et al.* 2000). Useful models for the last can be drawn from schools which already seem to be successful in particular contexts. Demie (2004) discusses the impact of good practice on black Caribbean students' achievement in Lambeth schools, while Driessen *et al.* (2004) show the importance of parental involvement to students' educational achievement but point out that parents from different social backgrounds view involvement with schools differently in the Netherlands. Many from ethnic minority backgrounds, they argue, find schools a foreign place and are unwilling to get involved with them. This in turn raises questions about the nature of the relationships that teachers might have with parents and what relationships of mutual respect and shared interest they may need to build to encourage greater parental involvement. Whatever practices and policies teachers implement in their schools, they need to monitor them especially to keep track of their impact on vulnerable students. One school in the study by Osler *et al.* (2000), with a large number of black and Asian origin students, did this and was able to reduce considerably the disproportionate use of punishments, such as fixed-term exclusions, with these students.

Central to the efforts of all 24 schools in a study by Osler *et al.* (2000) to develop more inclusive practices was their behaviour policies. They were adamant that such policies needed to be clear, consistent, fair and comprehensive. Policies were clear when they were understood by everybody in a school; when they gave unambiguous guidance to students and staff about what constitutes acceptable and unacceptable behaviour; when they made clear why particular types of behaviour were important and what punishments would occur if the rules of conduct were transgressed.

Consistent polices are those that are administered even-handedly among all those affected. Basic principles of honesty, respect, trust and hard work are expected of all staff and students. Behaviour issues are tackled in a simple, quick and efficient manner. So policies in schools are often enshrined in codes of practice and public morality offering institutional rules of action as well as being manifested in other rituals and language used by school members. These codes are often clearly displayed in every classroom and teachers draw students' attention to them to encourage them to work in certain ways and relate to people in certain ways. Marsh (1997) reported how students helped to build such codes of practice with the teachers in her school and how this engaged them with a positive approach to their behaviour that was based on intrinsic understanding of values rather than extrinsic rewards and punishments. For schools engaged in promoting improvement and inclusion, such codes might enshrine 'empathy, tolerance for diversity, and commitment to justice' (Ghosn 1998: 67) in a school or department committed to inclusivity and social justice. In one school the school code was the acronym TRUST, which emphasized 'Respect' for others and 'Standards of work' as well as 'Truthfulness' and 'Trust' in each other.

Policies are seen to be fair when they meet the strong sense of justice that children have and schools try to be even-handed in implementing behaviour policies, including students as much as possible in the process and in the solutions to problems. In these cases, schools reported (Osler *et al*. 2000) that students were much more likely to accept whatever judgements staff imposed. So codes of practice have to be applied in such a way as to take account of students' senses of justice/fairness of treatment, and try to reduce confrontations between students and staff. One school, for example, found that children were continually being told off on any one day by several staff for the same offence of breaking the uniform code, which was causing friction between staff and students. The school solved the problem by getting a student's form tutor to issue a 'uniform pass' for the day if the student arrived incorrectly dressed. Once the pass had been issued the incident was closed – and dealt with by the form tutor – so the student did not have to re-explain the circumstances to other staff (Osler *et al*. 2000). It also has to address conflict between students and students by introducing a firm anti-bullying policy and using student mentors.

Behaviour policies are comprehensive when they focus as much attention on managing the more serious types of misbehaviour and successive misbehaviours as on less serious types. Schools often have detailed procedures for the latter but not the former, especially if they have limited experience of challenging and vulnerable students. In some cases this results in schools running out of suitable interventions and strategies or resorting too quickly to the use of fixed-term or permanent exclusions.

A common theme in many schools facing student misbehaviour, especially that of a serious nature, is that it often begins with students' inabilities to access the curriculum successfully. This is a particular problem for students with learning difficulties and students who are not native speakers of English. In the study of Osler *et al*. (2000) one LA education officer suggested that schools need to address this by ensuring that the academic curriculum is delivered in a modern way, is kept up to date, is exciting, and 'is targeted so that there is an opportunity for students who are experiencing learning difficulties to have the same opportunity of access to the curriculum as the "high flyers"' (Osler *et al*. 2000: 23). Some LA officers in the study suggested that school transfer itself caused some students difficulties because of problems they experienced in adapting to the social expectations of their new schools. In one urban LA education officers indicated that there was a 38 per cent rise in exclusions in 1997/98 among pupils who transferred from inner-city primary schools to suburban secondary schools – parents often being encouraged to make this transfer because of the performance of the secondary schools in the local league tables.

In inclusive schools students are likely to be encouraged to take part in a variety of activities in and out of school, as well as developing their understandings of active citizenship through participating in school decision-making, as much through formal processes of involvement in a school's council as through learning how to take a responsible part in engaging with school during and outside lessons. However, such participation may be predicated on particular underlying cultural norms and precepts that depend on oral articulateness and various modes of interpersonal engagement that privilege some children from certain social backgrounds where such social capital (Bourdieu 1990) is constructed as a normal part of everyday life. The problem then is how to include those children without such social capital and how to create space for them to develop it.

An important element of a school's system for promoting inclusion is its pastoral education. This needs to focus as much on individual students' needs as on sustaining the systems of a school. It provides a series of arenas where staff can listen to why students act in the way they do and to understand where they are located socially and historically to make sense of the values that they hold. Knowledge of students' academic, personal and domestic circumstances provide staff with key indicators of problems and enable early intervention. These indicators might be dips in achievement, rise in absenteeism, domestic and family crises, changes in health, uncharacteristic behaviour, and bullying or being bullied. Good pastoral education in the schools in the study by Osler *et al.* (2000) noticeably reduced the number of exclusions given to students, particularly when it was used to identify and support those students who were most at risk of exclusion.

School support staff can be a useful agency for offering counselling or other support to students and parents and have the advantage for this role over teachers in that they are not obviously in an authority relationship with students. Librarians running learning support centres seem to have a particular part to play in this as their role is linked to student support in an informally structured learning environment. Contacts between staff and students in normal arenas such as classrooms and offices for discussions can be supplemented by withdrawal areas/'sanctuaries' that are supervised and 'time-out' opportunities for students under stress. There is, however, a risk that these sites become 'sin-bins' rather than part of a managed process for helping students to cope with school.

Fora have to be constructed where student and parent voices can be heard both formally and informally. The latter might take the form of using governors, perhaps particularly parent/community governors, in informal meetings with students and their parents to diffuse developing conflict situations before formal disciplinary proceedings are undertaken by getting students to explore possible solutions to a problem as well as their own contributions to it. 'Sanctuaries' and pupil referral units, especially those on the same site as the school that a student attends, can be used to contain and diffuse students with social and emotional difficulties which can be of significant advantage for the student, the school (some classes are no longer disrupted) and the community at large (students are not truanting and loitering around or getting involved in crime). However, these units are contentious for managing students' challenging behaviour and there are problems in sustaining them in terms of their costs and the integration of students' work in them with that of the rest of the school. Such units have to be carefully supervised to avoid them becoming sites where students perceive themselves as rejected from schooling, and so even less willing to engage positively with it, and further detached from the mainstream curriculum with which they may not be engaging successfully in any case.

Senior staff and teachers in schools cannot develop or implement inclusive practices and policies on their own. They need to work together as a community and with school support staff to develop whole-school approaches to inclusion. This is likely to involve them in partnerships with school governors, students, parents, local communities surrounding a school and eventually with a range of local authority services. The Children's Act (2004) in England and Wales helps to facilitate liaison between schools and other local authority agencies, not least by establishing them as part of one umbrella organization focused on children's welfare. Partnerships also need to extend to working with other schools in an area to track vulnerable students as well as with complementary schools (Martin *et al.* 2004). In the study by Osler *et al.* (2000) several secondary schools relied on information from the primary schools in their school families to transmit information to them about students' behavioural and academic needs, especially when they were 'at risk' children. In some cases at secondary school level, schools or schools and FE colleges were collaborating to allow students to have lessons in more than one school to reduce tension that they were experiencing in their personal relationships in one of them. It avoided students being excluded and losing contact with the formal academic curriculum.

7 Leading and constructing the curriculum

The national policy context

Knowledge is constructed socially through the uses of power by influential groups of people and individuals. Foucault (1975) points out how knowledge is constructed in different ways at different times and in different places, usually drawing on new technologies to legitimate changes in the construction of knowledge. A good example of this is how definitions of what should be taught to students in schools in England and Wales changed between the late 1960s and the early 1980s as various influential and powerful factions asserted their values for education by reshaping the national discourses about education. Eventually, in the early 1980s, these factions gained access to the legislative powers of central government and implemented a new definition of the school curriculum that ousted the power that teachers had wielded to construct it and assert their values since the 1944 Education Act.

As in many countries, such as the example of Saudi Arabia given in Chapter 2, the National Curriculum of England and Wales, set up in 1988, defined the purposes of education and what knowledge and skills school students should be taught as well as what counted as appropriate knowledge for them to be taught. In doing this central government heavily constrained what teachers could teach in schools. Since the early 1990s, through the programme of school inspection, and in the early twenty-first century, through the National Literacy and Numeracy strategies, central government has also tried to define how teachers should teach key elements of the formal academic curriculum in schools.

The National Curriculum is defined in terms of both academic subjects and personal and social criteria for students' development. The Education Reform Act (ERA) 1988 asserts the importance of two goals for a balanced and broadly based curriculum:

The promotion of the spiritual, moral, cultural, mental and physical development of pupils at the school and of society

The preparation of pupils for the opportunities, responsibilities and experiences of adult life

(Section 1, para. 2)

This is emphasized in the Teachers' Guide to the National Curriculum (1989). Table 7.1 sets out the academic subjects to be delivered by the National Curriculum, indicating which are core subjects that are given a disproportionate amount of time in each school's timetable because of their perceived importance to national society, and which other subjects must be taught. The inclusion of RE (religious education) in a largely Christian framework is evidence of the historic influence of the Church of England over education in England and Wales, rather than a reasonable reflection of the current multi-faith nature of society in England and Wales. In addition foundation subjects must be taught, but should only take up what time is available after the core subjects have been given adequate provision.

Table 7.1 The National Curriculum of England and Wales

Subjects that must be taught	Core subjects	Foundation subjects	Cross-curriculum (see Table 7.2)
RE	English	History	Dimensions
Citizenship	Maths	Geography	Themes
(since 2002)	Science	Technology	Skills
		Modern Languages	
		PE	
		Music	
		Art	

Since the year 2000 a pre-school or foundation stage curriculum has been specified for children below the age of 5 years, when formal schooling starts in England and Wales.

As well as specific subjects, a variety of cross-curriculum skills and areas of knowledge, which are usually taught through other subjects, have been specified for children to learn, as is shown in Table 7.2. Since 2002 Citizenship, one of these themes, has to have space on each school's timetable as a subject in its own right. Since the Children's Act (2004) a variety of transferable skills have been proposed by central government which all schools will have to deliver as part of the curriculum when the Act is fully implemented.

Table 7.2 Cross-curriculum themes and skills for the National Curriculum

Dimensions	Themes	Skills
Equal opportunities	Economic and industrial	Communication
Multi-cultural	Health	(literacy/oracy)
Personal and social	Careers	Numeracy
development	Environment	Study skills
	Citizenship	Problem solving
		Information technology
		Personal and social
		development

Certain aspects of this curriculum have to be delivered by teachers at particular levels for children at certain ages or stages of the National Curriculum – see Table 7.3. Students at these ages and stages are expected to perform competently at these levels, and failure to do so is taken as a measure by OFSTED of a school's inadequacy to deliver effective teaching and learning. There are four such stages, called Key Stages, the first two equating to the primary phase of schooling and the second two to the secondary phase. The assessment of the academic elements of this curriculum have also been specified by central government. Children of particular ages coincident with the oldest age group in each Key Stage have to take Standard Assessment Tests (SATs) and are expected to achieve at particular levels or standards of performance which are specified by central government for that Key Stage. This completely ignores a weight of research-based evidence about the variability of children's physical, emotional and intellectual development, putting slower developing children at risk of being incorrectly labelled as underachievers academically. At Key Stage 4, which equates to the years during which students prepare for their school leaving examinations – the GCSE (General Certificate of Secondary Education) – the SATs are replaced by the individual subject examinations that make up the GCSE.

Table 7.3 Ages and stages of the National Curriculum

Key Stage	Foundation	1	2	3	4*
Students' ages	< 5 years	5–7 years	7–11 years	11–14 years	14–16 years
School years		1–2	3–6	7–9	10–11
SATs		Year 2	Year 6	Year 9	Year 11
School type	Nursery/ pre-school	Primary/ infant	Primary/ junior	Secondary	

Note: *This is taken as GCSE or equivalent vocational courses for GNVQ level 2.

Such is the detail in which the curriculum and the targets for performance are defined by central government that it is easy to perceive this curriculum as in effect a syllabus for which teachers can – and are expected to – construct lesson plans. This impression is enhanced by the number of school textbooks that have been written specifically to help teachers deliver the National Curriculum.

In the early twenty-first century central government tightened its control on how teachers can practise by introducing literacy and numeracy strategies, initially for primary schools, to improve the quality of learning and teaching in these subjects, and a Key Stage 3 strategy to guide teachers in their practices with students of this age. These strategies were not evaluated before implementation but recent (2005) anecdotal evidence suggests that they have been unsuccessful in raising the quality of learning, but very successful in depressing student and teacher enthusiasm for the subjects.

Teachers are responsible for working with students to help them learn what has been defined as knowledge by a school's curriculum. The formal curriculum includes all those activities designed or encouraged within a school's organizational framework to promote the intellectual, personal, social and physical development of its students. The informal and social aspects of the curriculum occur by osmosis as students and staff interact in the construction and re-construction of school communities to create cultures of student learning and engagement with schooling; student participation in the social processes of schooling; less student disaffection; greater student social and learning skills; wider teachers' repertoires of formal and informal strategies for working with students to meet the needs of a variety of different students, including those with particular educational needs.

Developing a critical perspective

How the state wields power over education and student development through the bodies of its school children and teachers (Foucault 1977) is through the construction of the National Curriculum and its assessment. This constrains the power of students, teachers and senior staff in schools to act autonomously. The construction and policing by central government agencies, such as the DfES, of school league tables, of school performance measured in terms of examination results and of parental choice of schools, are three major mechanisms for sustaining surveillance of teachers' work. How well students perform in SATs and public examinations in England and Wales affects the esteem in which schools are held locally and nationally since these results are published as national league tables. These indicators of school and student performance are published as raw scores, taking no account of how social and economic factors affect children's educational achievement at local level. Nor do they take account of the value that schools might have added to students' performance whatever raw score level of performance they might have achieved. Fielding (2001) considers scathingly the impact of performance indicators on people in schools, whether students or teachers, and doubts that they really measure what people achieve while offering a mechanism for government bureaucracies and senior staff in schools to impose control on others.

As a result of central government policy school concerns with students' performances have become increasingly corporate, viewing the student as a producer of results to meet the interests of the school as organization. In the neo-liberal and quasi-economic framework that dominates national discourses about society, and about education as part of that, knowledge seems to be defined as a product from a factory process (like a computer) called schooling rather than as a sense-making process through which people create understandings of the different worlds around them, be they physical, emotional, moral, spiritual, social, aesthetic or intellectual. The intrinsic value of education for helping people to develop as individuals and develop social and cultural capital (Bourdieu 1990) that will allow them to pursue what opportunities they want to in society appears to be of decreasing importance in these discourses on education in which the importance of education as a means of constructing social control is emphasized.

Within the framework of the National Curriculum and state direction of pedagogy teachers have become increasingly defined as the deliverers of a syllabus prescribed by central government, the quality of their performance being measured by OFSTED evaluations since 1993. Through the reports of its inspectors and the criteria for evaluating schools it has published, OFSTED has made clear what it believes constitutes effective teaching. Both central government and its agencies, such as OFSTED, propose a single model for successful teaching that is claimed to be suitable for all circumstances regardless of the students with whom the teachers have to work, and regardless of the extensive research that points to the influence of students' social and economic backgrounds, gender and ethnicity on their engagement with learning (Thrupp 1998; Francis and Archer 2005; Kazmi and Hallan 2005) and their ability to adapt to a variety of school contexts particularly as these are manifested in different school cultures.

Such an approach overlooks a number of important factors that affect teaching–learning processes at the local or institutional level. One of these is the extent to which the curriculum is adapted to the needs of the students in a particular location or socio-economic context and so the extent to which the curriculum is equally accessible to all students. As a special education needs coordinator (SENCO) explained in the study by Osler *et al.* (2000), a common strand across many schools was that 'for the majority of children at high risk of exclusion because of their behaviour [we] can trace it back to a learning difficulty which is about being able to access the work or frustration at not being able to spell or read and often literacy problems' (SENCO, primary school).

Another is that students' views on schooling and the learning–teaching process are not heard. Such views are, of course, mediated by gender, socio-economic status and ethnicity. Ranson (2000) discusses the importance of listening to students' voices, the social construction of students' views by students, if students, especially those already marginalized by various social processes, are to avoid being further excluded and disadvantaged socially through their engagement or, more accurately, lack of engagement with the school system. Ranson (2000) argues that exclusion from school and from the curriculum at whatever level is a denial of citizenship. It is for schools, he argues, to help students develop a critical voice so they can make the most of the opportunities schools offer. Flutter and Rudduck (2004) take the argument a step further, pointing out that this level of engagement in schools is essential if students are to experience schools as democratic institutions reflecting the wider democratic structures and processes of society in England and Wales, i.e. for the rhetoric of citizenship in the curriculum to be enacted and learnt by students through their experiences. However, Fielding (2004) acknowledges that developing the practice of hearing student voices is problematic because it challenges current distributions of power in schools if it is to be introduced effectively rather than cosmetically. It raises questions about how people are able to present themselves, in what arenas they are able to speak for themselves (see Cribb and Gewirtz 2003, in Chapter 10) and which policies and practices existing organizational and social power structures permit them to discuss and influence. Allowing student voices to be heard successfully means they have to speak directly in the dialogues normally dominated by staff and powerful members of staff about the construction of the school as a community (Fielding 2004). This view is closely related to that discussed in Chapter 6 on the introduction of cultures of inclusion in schools.

A third factor is that teachers belong to various epistemic communities which influence their views on what constitutes successful teaching and learning in those communities (subject areas; students of particular ages) and what resources are needed to achieve that. So teachers are influenced in their construction of educational knowledge by agencies and people perceived as influential custodians of social definitions of legitimate knowledge: not only by central government views, but by those of subject associations to which they belong, by contacts with other teachers of the same subject or age group of students, by academic histories (e.g. the university they attended and what they were taught in particular departments there), and by the media. These sources of influence might be contacted in various ways by teachers looking for information on how to construct knowledge with students or be thrust at teachers by agents of these agencies as they try to assert their perspectives over teachers.

Two other aspects that this instrumentally focused model of the curriculum enshrined in the National Curriculum overlooks are discussed in other chapters. One is the impact of the social and cultural mix that students bring with them to school which affects strongly the ethos or culture of the school that they help to construct along with the staff of the school, especially the more powerful and influential staff. That culture shapes the particular sense of community that emerges in a school. The other aspect is the importance and values embedded in the culture itself that is constructed and, consequently, the informal social and emotional curriculum that is learnt by students and promulgated by staff. This affects considerably the quality of cooperation that staff are able to build with students and their parents or carers and the local communities of whatever sort from which they are drawn, and the other educational institutions near them.

Constructing an accessible formal curriculum

Schools make a difference by addressing social inequalities through providing a 'supportive, caring school environment that focuses on students ... [so that] all students can learn under appropriate circumstances ... [that] emphasize individual effort for all students ... to ensure that each achieves the highest standards possible ..., facilitates adaptive patterns of cognition, affect and behaviour ..., [makes sure] students are engaged ... [and] teachers are effective' (Raham 2003: 6). Her study looked at 12 urban schools in low-income districts in Canada which all served multi-cultural populations and were required to give priority of access to students living in their catchment areas, although she notes that they were in competition with other public and private schools in their areas. Slee (1991: 57) suggests that schools that successfully promote children's engagement have the following:

- a clearly articulated philosophy or statement of goals
- clear patterns of formal and informal communications
- democratic decision-making processes
- systematic attention to student records (to enhance performance rather than as a surveillance mechanism)
- parents involved as helpers, teachers and in decision-making, and students working in projects outside the school
- school resources were available and used
- students and teachers worked together to improve the school environment
- senior staff took responsibility for ensuring that teachers' morale was high.

A clear coherent philosophy for a school constructed and endorsed by its staff, students and parents is of key importance as are the values embedded in it which are projected through institutional policies and practices. Riley (2004) indicates that a school's philosophy may be secular – contained in its vision and mission statement, perhaps – or indicated by its faith traditions where it is a faith-based school. For example, Guru Nanak Secondary School in west London received an excellent report from OFSTED in 2003 and was complimented on how its faith-based philosophy of serving others had percolated the ways in which students and teachers worked with each other in school and addressed issues of gender discrimination in local communities out of school (*TES*, 28 March 2003).

Schools and classrooms are sites for debating and developing particular values as well as particular constructions of knowledge and also act as conduits through which some values and knowledge, rather than others, are transmitted. Teachers are responsible for enacting this with their students in moral ways. Moral ways are those norms and values that are sanctioned by society and frame the ways in which teachers are expected by national and local society to interact with students. Fullan (2003) sees moral imperatives operating at every level within a school because the intention of schooling is to benefit students in terms of desirable identifiable goals and particular cultures of social and economic relationships in which are embedded certain values, whether or not these are clearly articulated. Unfortunately the assumption of homogeneity of morality between national society and its multiplicity of local communities and institutions, a view put forward by Hofstede (1991) in his discussion of linkages between national and institutional cultures, cannot be sustained, since each community and institution develops its own culture encapsulating norms and beliefs that reflect the core values and identities of it members as well as national cultural values to some extent. Consequently teachers are left facing a multiplicity of demands on how they construct the curriculum with their students that reflect the multiplicity of views from the different communities that their school serves.

The scope of this problem directly translates into how teachers manage the curriculum. In schools where teachers have overtly discussed with students various teaching models and strategies, students are able to understand the appropriateness of the use of different approaches to pedagogy (Beresford 2003). He found that such discussions helped students and teachers to develop a shared culture in which they were not afraid to ask for help and to ask for help appropriately not only about how to learn but how well they were learning (p. 4). Such a culture, it seemed, helped students to hone their own assessments of their performances, helping them to develop their autonomy as learners. It was helped by the availability of mentors for students and of teachers willing to see students privately after classes to discuss work. Providing time for such tutorial work has implications for the organization of a school as well as for teachers' workloads.

However, to ensure that a school's curriculum allows students experiencing learning difficulties to have the same access to it as gifted and talented students requires more than staff just talking and working with their students – and their students' parents and carers – it also needs staff in schools to acknowledge the cultural heritages of the students in their schools however these are shaped by socio-economic status, gender or ethnicity. Coles and Chilvers (2005) point out that the DfES consultation document *Aiming High* (2003) was concerned that students from Black and Pakistani and Bangladeshi backgrounds were performing less well at GCSE than students from other ethnic groups, a view borne out by Kazmi and Hallan (2005), and that LEAs and schools were required to address this problem in the construction of their Educational or School Development Plans. One cause of this under performance may be that the content of the National Curriculum of England and Wales contains insufficient culturally relevant examples for many students from ethnic minority and faith groups. Another is that students in school often lack the opportunity to use their heritage languages as part of the curriculum or for students from various cultural heritages to learn at least some of each other's languages. Both show a lack of recognition of and valuing of students' cultural heritages, discouraging students from identifying positively with schools as a central part of their social lives. This in turn is likely to inhibit their learning, as Willis (1977) demonstrated in his study many years ago.

To address this issue Coles and Chilvers (2005) argue that school staff need to develop a culturally inclusive curriculum. This will help students of all ethnic and faith backgrounds to develop an affinity with their schools, so building a sense of engagement with schooling because it helps students to feel that their own cultural perspectives are valued and not merely being subsumed under a centralizing educational discourse that privileges particular values and cultural practices. Such an approach allows students to sustain legitimately a multiplicity of identities and build bridges between those, for example those who are British (born in Britain perhaps of parents born in Britain) but also of Indian heritage or of Muslim faith. Encouraging students to choose one rather than enjoying the richness growing from several causes social and emotional conflict for students, possibly provoking them to act in socially unacceptable ways when they are not sure how to meet the contradictory expectations of them (Benjamin 2002). This also points to the need for schools to create the time and space for students of different faiths to engage in their religious practices and for other students in a school to understand what these are and why they are considered important by members of that faith. Donnelly (2004) discusses the importance and processes of constructing such a tolerant approach in multi-faith schools in Northern Ireland.

The development of such aspects of a school's curriculum, however, take time and other resources to construct them. Teachers need time to research the materials that are suitable for supporting the diverse cultural heritages of students as well as to discuss with parents and leaders of the communities that a school serves what aspects of their cultures they want enacted. The way that time is allocated to activities by those people such as senior staff in a school able to define this indicates the values a school projects and makes that time not available for other activities. Constructing a timetable for a school places senior staff in a powerful position to embedded values, including those of celebrating cultrual diversity, in the curriculum. Within its matrix of time and space teachers and students have to work. Students' access to particular slots in time and space in the school day not only shaped their interactions with teachers but with other students, too. Ireson and Hallam (2001) point out that how students are allocated to classes, whether through setting or streaming by academic ability, gives them an indication of how valued they are by teachers, since it establishes a hierarchy of expected performance however carefully teachers disguise this. Whether or not such discrimination really improves performance seems questionable, but there is a real risk that students will perform to the level apparently expected of them by the teaching groups to which they are allocated.

Other resources that teachers are likely to need in a multi-cultural school are also cultural or linguistic resources, which teachers in a school may not have, to help staff use culturally appropriate material successfully. It points to the importance of schools bringing in local community members to help with these aspects, perhaps involving parents in such matters. Vincent (2000) argues that involving members of a school's local community in these ways helps to improve their engagement with schooling and raise the quality of learning undertaken by their children.

Another means by which students' heritage backgrounds can be addressed educationally is through formal schools working closely with any complementary schools that might be providing aspects of the curriculum that a mainstream school cannot provide because it does not have the resources available (Coles and Chilvers 2005; Martin *et al.* 2004). Complementary schools, sometimes called supplementary schools, are voluntary schools that are usually set up by a local community to meet the educational needs of its children in its particular culture, whether this focuses on learning knowledge about its cultural heritage, its faith heritage or its linguistic heritage. The research by Martin *et al.* (2004) found that such schools in their study were soundly run and expected their students to take their work seriously, often expecting them, where appropriate, to work towards public examinations in the knowledge taught and achieve results at as high a standard as possible. They noted, as did Coles and Chilvers (2005), that such schools seemed to build up students' self-confidence as learners because they could relate their learning to their social lives and were given parental support and public recognition for their attendance, performance and achievement in them. However, there can be conflicting demands on students' time if complementary schools and mainstream schools are both expecting them to contribute an amount of study time outside the hours of schooling.

Students who struggle to access the curriculum successfully may do so for several reasons. This chapter does not have the space to discuss such a topic in detail but sketches in some of the main points here of students' struggles to assert their agency when school systems may be particularly unaccommodating. It raises questions about how teachers can avert these conflicts through the ways in which they construct the curriculum with their students. The hostility and frustration such conflict generates can be a major cause of students underachieving in schools in various ways and of social and behavioural confrontations with teachers that prevent students engaging positively with schooling.

One of the causes of students gaining inadequate access to the curriculum is the result of language difficulties – having insufficient command of English, particularly if they are relatively newly arrived in Britain. The provision of learning support staff who are bi-lingual in the relevant languages along with English language classes for the students can ameliorate this. Another cause is the variety of learning difficulties that some students may have or experience at least for a while. Central government policy tried to address this in schools in England and Wales by creating a framework for the provision of a range of Special Educational Needs support in the Education Act of 1993 and the Special Educational Needs code of practice that was promulgated in 1994. For some students at Key Stage 4 with some emotional and behavioural difficulties and in some local government authorities there is provision for some students, in certain circumstances, to attend technical colleges or schools in addition to their own school to take courses that are specifically relevant to their needs or intended career plans (Osler *et al.* 2000). Yet other reasons that students struggle to access the curriculum can be various emotional and social traumas that they are experiencing at some point in time as a result of any number of possible life experiences. Osler *et al.* (2000) argue that the development of pupil referral units, especially where they are on the same site as the school that a student usually attends, help to give students a place where they can temporarily escape from the tensions they are experiencing but remain in contact with the curriculum.

Constructing the social curriculum

If teachers' construction of the academic curriculum with students is heavily constrained in state schools in England and Wales by the National Curriculum and the other aspects of central government education policy, they have far more freedom to construct a social curriculum with their students. However, this curriculum is bounded by the cultural norms and beliefs of the macro-society and the local communities in which teachers' schools are embedded.

Whatever is done to make more accessible the academic, physical and aesthetic aspects of the curriculum to students, it is unlikely to be successful if it merely addresses instrumental matters of time, space and resources and does not consider the quality of relationships developed between staff and students. Although teachers are of major importance in this process as well as in the provision of engaging pedagogy so, too, are the midday supervisors and other support staff who regularly interact with students and sometimes their parents. The quality of staff relationships with students that seem to be successful in helping students to have a positive attitude to schooling are said by Hopkins *et al.* (1997b: 10) to have the following qualities:

- authentic relationships – the quality of openness and congruence of relationships existing in the classroom
- boundaries and expectations – the pattern of expectations set by the teacher and the school of student performance and behaviour within the classroom
- planning for teaching – the access of teachers to a range of pertinent teaching materials and the ability to plan and differentiate these materials for a range of students
- teaching repertoire – the range of teaching styles and models available for use by a teacher, dependent on student, context curriculum and desired outcome
- pedagogic partnerships – the ability of teachers to form professional relationships within and outside the classroom that focus on the study and improvement of practice
- reflection on teaching – the capacity of the individual teacher to reflect on his or her own practice, and to put to the test of practice specifications of teaching from other sources.

These qualities generate mutual respect between staff and students and a willingness for staff to listen carefully to students' voices, however uncomfortable may be some of the things that they say, and work with students to implement an agreed culture. This culture is based on justice and equity – codes that bind student behaviour being equally applicable to staff – and an agreed agenda of teaching and learning in the classroom.

Many disaffected students find school a sad and worrying experience. Some are worried about doing badly in class or in examinations and then getting into trouble from teachers and parents for it. Others find school a tedious experience with school work being perceived as boring or incomprehensible (Riley and Rustique-Forrester 2002). The main importance for some of these students in coming to school is to be with their friends, regardless of what they achieve academically. And many of them, as both Benjamin (2002) and Riley and Rustique-Forrester (2002) report, do not expect to achieve much at school because of the way they have been marginalized either from the main processes of schooling by setting or streaming, or being placed in special classes or units, or because they have no hope of achieving those benchmarks that the school set as targets for students to gain positive recognition.

If students have a clear view of what is poor quality teaching and schooling, they also seem to have a clear view of what is good quality. An example of their views on this are set out in Table 7.4. However, they also have a broader understanding of what constitutes successful schooling. As part of a research project on schooling in disadvantaged areas, Grace *et al.* (1996) reported on a school in Cleveland that was considered to be effective by OFSTED. They found students welcomed being in a school with strong support in the local community from parents and other community-based organizations. They welcomed being in a caring and ordered community, an ethos, in this case, derived from Roman Catholic and Christian values, although the school was a state comprehensive school. This manifested itself in part in the quality of the buildings and work environment on which students commented enthusiastically.

Table 7.4 Students' perceptions of 'good' and 'bad' teachers

'Good' teachers	'Bad' teachers
Helpful and supportive	Mean and unfair
Taking the time to explain material in depth	Unwilling to help or explain material and ideas beyond instruction
Friendly and personable	Judgemental of pupils' [sic] parents and
Understandings and know the subject well	siblings
Using a variety of teaching styles and innovative approaches	Routine and unchanging in their teaching styles and methods
Fair and having equal standards and expectations of pupils, regardless of their test scores	Inflexible and disrespectful of pupils [sic] Unaware of and unsympathetic to pupils' personal problems
Willing to regard pupils for progress	Physically intimidating and verbally abusive

(source: Riley and Rustique-Forrester 2002: 30)

It also manifests itself in the way in which teachers are willing to become involved with students in a variety of activities outside those formally conducted in the classroom. Students welcomed this and the way that the pastoral care system and organization of student groups academically acknowledged the dignity of the individual. The discipline system was perceived by students as strict but fair, but Grace *et al.* (1996) claimed that it worked in a low-key manner: students approved of the way in which the school was led, perceiving the teachers and head teacher as working collaboratively together, and the head teacher being clearly visible both in the school and as a teacher. They remarked favourably on his enthusiasm for supporting them and their concerns, and for promoting a positive public image of their school. They were proud to be part of a school that was successful academically and sportingly and that advertised this to the local community. This is in sharp contrast to the views of students in schools said to be failing by OFSTED, who thought they were of little worth because the school had failed its inspection (Benjamin 2002; Busher and Barker 2003).

Part of this social curriculum is helping students to develop as autonomous learners who spend some time working in groups and problem-solving or in independent activities during formal lessons. According to Beresford (2003), students welcome this sense of independence since it helps to give them a sense of ownership of their work. However, this requires teachers to move from delivering knowledge to students to becoming expert in guiding students to build up their conceptual understanding of a subject. This, in turn, gives students the tools to make choices and decisions about what constitutes successful learning and how to evaluate that. Teachers also have to give students training in how to learn successfully in different ways, for example developing an appreciation of what are more and less successful modes of group work, and how those ways can be monitored effectively. Beresford (2003) points out that if students are not helped to acquire the learning skills needed for independent learning they can waste a lot of time and generate a lot of disruptive behaviour. Joyce *et al.* (1997) point out that different people have different preferred approaches to learning and so will learn more effectively if they are using these.

Another part is the quality of relationships that teachers develop with their students. Students are especially appreciative of teachers who take a personal interest in them and their development (Busher 2002; Beresford 2003). They seem to develop stronger collaborative working relationships with such teachers, at least in England and Wales. What would constitute appropriate teacher–student relationships in other and non-anglophone or non-western cultures needs to be researched carefully. These positive relationships are especially important for allowing teachers to develop trust with students and build up students' positive views of whatever subject it is on which they are working. This allows teachers and students to develop a clear perspective on students' competence at particular subjects or topics within subjects unclouded by distractions about the quality of relationship between teacher and student.

Such relationships seem to be powerfully constructed when students claim to experience a sense of justice in the moral codes and practices of a school and in the way its lessons are managed and its corridors policed. Marsh (1997) suggested that one way to help generate this was for teachers to negotiate the rules of behaviour for their classes with their students. Having been involved in developing such rules, she claimed students were much more willing to accept such rules and to enforce them. Consequently the behaviours and interpersonal relationships that teachers model not only with students but also with their colleagues, especially in public arenas such as corridors, is important in helping to form such a culture in a school. Day *et al.* (2000) suggested that the interpersonal skills of senior staff as well as teaching and support staff were an important element in helping shape students' views of schooling.

Yet another part of this social curriculum is empowering students' voices. Since 2002 central government in England and Wales has required schools to set up school councils to provide a forum where students can express their views on how their school is managed and make suggestions about how its social structures might be modified. This is projected as part of central government policy to teach citizenship in schools, giving students the opportunity to experience engaging in some of the consultative processes that they are likely to experience in the macro-society as adults. It is supposed to allow students to help shape the policies of a school but in view of the pressures on schools to meet targets of performativity and the tight constraints that schools face from central government on the construction of the curriculum and on pedagogy, it is possible that it will only serve to make more visible to students the limits of their and their teachers' influence over the curriculum and other aspects of school policy and so engender more rapidly the cynicism about consultative processes that many of their adult colleagues have already acquired when schools are managed in certain ways (Busher and Saran 1992).

Building partnerships with parents

A key aspect of developing the social curriculum in a school is for staff to build positive and mutually supportive partnerships with parents. Closer relationships between parents and schools seem to raise the quality of work in the classroom (Carney 2004). In part this may be because of parental acceptance of a school's philosophy as manifested in its codes of practice and vision of what is involved in being a member of the school community

(Shaw 2003). In part it may be because schools are able to find a variety of ways of involving parents working in schools voluntarily or in a paid capacity, either in the classroom, directly supporting learning, or in a work room preparing resources, or in a clerical capacity – or using other skills that they possess. It can also involve schools finding space for parents to use rooms for meetings and social intercourse during the school day or using other school facilities such as accessing the internet (Nesbitt 2004) when these are not needed by students. The value of joint-use facilities, such as sports centres, to schools and local communities is widely recognized especially in those rural areas where only such provision makes it economic for both school and community to have these facilities. It encourages parents to develop a sense of ownership of a school.

Helping parents to engage with schools to support the development of their children is a much broader perspective than encouraging them to support a school's homework policy or to support a school's behaviour policy under the Home School Agreements Guidance (DfEE 1998). Agreements set up under this scheme to date seem only to be bland monitoring devices (Ouston and Hood 2000) which have tended to be gender and race blind. Crozier (2000) complains that the model put forward by this guidance assumes that all parents have the same needs when working with schools and their children can be treated in the same ways. The problem is greater for those children who do not have parents but are reliant on carers, and often a shifting collection of carers, to look after their interests with schools.

Helping parents to engage with schools, then, has to take account of the diversity of their backgrounds, ethnically, linguistically, culturally, socially and educationally. Osler *et al.* (2000) found that the parents of a school in a very disadvantaged urban area, many of whom were recently arrived in England, had little idea of what was involved in schooling in England, a weak grasp of English, and a limited understanding of various aspects of the curriculum or of central government policy on that curriculum. As a result they were not able to give guidance to their children on how to engage successfully with the school. Faced with the problem, the school ran a series of classes for parents, either as informal seminars or as one-on-one discussions, so that they could understand what schooling in England involved and what was required of and offered to them and their children. In another LEA in the 1990s, schools ran a series of computer clubs, which were said by education officers to be very popular, to help parents develop their IT skills and understand what help their children needed in developing their IT skills.

However, parental participation can be potentially threatening to professional control of a school, especially when parental views are at odds with the manifested values and cultures of a school or when there are a diversity of values and views in the parent body (Crozier 2000). This may explain why schools try to engage with parents in a variety of different ways, only some of which might be construed as a genuine partnership of teachers and parents. Vincent (2000) presents several models of relationships between parents and schools. The most limited of these models is what she terms the independent model (p. 2) where there is little communication or interaction between parent and school except for formal communications. Slightly more engaged is the model of parent as consumer, when parents are encouraged to hold the school to account for its actions in promoting their children's learning. This is the model favoured by central government through its use of league tables and its assumption that students' learning outcomes are strongly correlated mainly with the quality of teaching they receive, a view that is hotly disputed by many educational and school effectiveness researchers such as Creemers (1994). More engaged still is the parent as supporter of the school who is coached by school staff to support the teachers and the school as organization by, for example, taking part in school educational events and fund-raising drives.

The most engaged model is that of parent as participant which Vincent (2000) sees as fostering citizenship among parents as they are expected to play an equal part with school-based professionals in shaping the development of the school. The last model, of collective entitlement to engagement with education, sits uncomfortably with neo-liberal perspectives and the more limited models of consumerist engagement with education that central government in the early twenty-first century has espoused. It overlooks the range of social and cultural capital that different parents have and raises questions about how far it potentially discriminates against those who lack the capital to engage fully in such deliberative and democratic approaches to running schools. Unless handled sensitively, the risk is that a school promoting this model will make parents not able to subscribe to it feel inadequate. So teachers need to find ways of accepting and welcoming parents to join in with school that recognizes the differences that parents bring to that task and helps them to understand more clearly how they and their children can engage successfully with it.

8 Developing cultures of learning in subject areas

The core of leadership in schools: creating cultures of learning

People are not islands in institutions but part of collectivities (Lukes 1974), such as schools, school subject departments or year groups of students, which have their own particular sub-cultures or small cultures that reflect the norms, beliefs and values supported by members of such groups and to which their members are expected to subscribe. Such sub-cultures, especially those in secondary schools in England, may also be in conflict with the wider institutional culture, as Siskin (1991) has shown. Cultures establish norms and expectations for action and decision-making for each department, group or community which are as binding on their leaders as they are on other members of the department or community – see Figure 8.1 (page 121). This coincides with Lukes' (1974) view of the importance of collective power that exists alongside the power and influence of individuals. The cultures that leaders create with their colleagues become symbols of collective identity for the members of each collectivity, in this case their pastoral and academic departments of secondary schools which are normally led by people who are often designated as subject or middle leaders.

Organizational sub-cultures are manifested in various ways: through the ways in which middle leaders make available to departmental colleagues knowledge and resources; through the language they use when speaking to colleagues, students and other people; through the ways in which they demonstrate their own concern, or lack of it, for being well organized and prepared for teaching the students; through the ceremonies of formal meetings they hold; through the ways in which they involve colleagues, or do not involve them, in decision-making – making manifest the extent to which colleagues' views are valued. When successful these cultures help teachers develop an attachment to their departments even though teachers and support staff will always disagree to some extent with the cultures and policies being created by middle leaders when these do not fit their own preferred views.

Figure 8.1 A socially constructed view of a 'good' middle leader

Norms and beliefs of members of a department:
- a successful teacher – make learning interesting
- an advocate for colleagues
- knowledgeable about the curriculum
- good at controlling students
- well organized personally/professionally
- supportive of department colleagues
- caring for/of students
- effective at implementing senior management policy
- 'an effective manager' has a vision for the department.

(source: Busher 2005a)

The sub-cultures created by middle leaders studied by Busher (2002) seem to have been quasi-collegial like those recommended by Hopkins (2001) as being necessary for improving schooling in England, although they probably did not fulfil the strict notions for genuine collegiality that Hargreaves (1994) put forward, as the hierarchical relationships between middle leaders and teachers was always visible and openly acknowledged by teachers and middle leaders. However, other leaders in other schools and departments might create different cultures and sub-cultures which would have different impacts on the ways in which teachers might be willing to work together.

Constructing a learning community

One conceptual framework for understanding the dynamic interactions that take place in subject and pastoral departments is the notion of professional learning communities. These are communities of practice in schools that focus on fostering learning with students, be it in academic subjects or in personal and social development. Clark (1996) perceived such communities as social systems that have a purpose, the members of which fulfil a diversity of roles within a recognizable and sustainable collectivity. Senge (1990) perceived learning communities as sites where people expand their capacities to work in new and creative ways through working together, a not unreasonable description of what takes place in schools.

This raises a question about who has membership of a school or work-related learning community. In many departments in secondary schools not only teachers have membership of them, but support staff, too. Indeed earlier research by Busher and Blease (2000) suggests that support staff play an important part in the construction of a school as an organization or community and are an integral element of many departmental teams. As

Greenfield (1993: 103) points out, 'organizations are accomplished by people and people are responsible for what goes on in them'. Learning communities in schools have to encompass all the potential members of them. Ethnographic interest in multiple voices in organizations is part epistemological and part ethical (Linstead 1993: 53). These voices include the support staff, teachers, students and their carers or parents, and governors – although the extent to which parents can be said to be part of a school organization is debatable (Gray 1991). Students do the work of creating knowledge through their learning and contribute informally to the construction of the social framework of a school, while the teachers, support staff and parents or carers lead, manage and support the students in these activities. Bottery (2003) rejects the notion of learning communities being exclusive on grounds of race, religion or finance. In these circumstances, to label learning communities as 'professional' seems at best confusing and at worst an indication of some covert exclusivity – restricted to the professional members of a school, presumably the teachers, although some other staff might claim membership, too. For the rest of this chapter these communities of practice are simply referred to as 'learning communities'.

Such learning communities can be as large as a whole school or as small as a classroom, or a subject department or pastoral area in a secondary school in England. Senge (1990) perceived learning communities as sites where people expand their capacities to work in new and creative ways through working together. Smylie (1994) thought they have collaborative cultures, allowing teachers to work interdependently to promote student learning. Louis *et al.* (1996) point out the importance of members sharing values and of reflective dialogue to improve practice. It implies a culture of trust between members (Blase and Blase 1994) that allows them to take risks, perhaps through sharing ideas and receiving constructive feedback from colleagues. Such a culture allows teachers, support staff and students to tackle complex problems as effectively as possible (Hargreaves 1994) by building on existing expertise, pooling resources and providing each other with moral support. It revolves around social values that emphasize an awareness of others and is a key part in developing the distinctive collaborative cultures of learning communities shown in Figure 8.2 (page 123).

Schools as learning communities and learning communities in schools are in part shaped by their formal leaders and in part by the members of them. Where they develop collaborative cultures it is through people working together and engaging in rigorous reflection on the values they espouse and enact (Schon 1987). Leaders tend to be more influential than their colleagues in shaping these cultures because of their greater access to various sources of power – see Chapter 4 – but to construct the collaborative cultures that seem to help learning communities to develop they need to have awareness of and sympathy with the social, emotional and work-related needs of staff colleagues. To some extent this awareness may

Figure 8.2 Key attributes of a learning school/organization

Key attributes:
- the willingness of staff to reflect and discuss what is being done in teaching and learning
- the development of a collective focus by staff on student learning
- the development of shared norms and values
- an openness to innovation and reasonable risk taking
- staff empowerment: autonomy within an agreed organizational framework.

These are brought about in part by:
- having time to meet and discuss
- the development of trust and respect among colleagues
- supportive leadership
- a deepening professional knowledge by staff of pedagogy, curriculum (subject area), and organizational process.

(source: Wallace *et al.* 1997)

depend on who they are as people, their personhood (Aubrey *et al.* 2000), and the values they project through that – in other words on the identities they have constructed for themselves in their past and present interactions with other people (Giddens 1991). Bottery (2003) points out that vigorous learning communities inevitably invite their members to develop critical perspectives of the impact that external social, organizational, political and economic contexts have on the ways in which they work and would like to work.

How access to sources of power is used affects the relationships between middle leaders and their colleagues and shapes the decisions that are taken and the ways in which they can be implemented. Middle leaders using power with or through people (Blase and Anderson 1995) tend to enable colleagues and students to enhance their positive work-related identities and engage collaboratively with their work. If power is used manipulatively rather than facilitatively then leaders are likely to promote corporatism (Tannenbaum and Schmidt 1973), however soft the means they may be using, and cynicism among staff.

An important element of learning communities is that their cultures empower their members creatively to develop themselves and their performance of practice. Murphy (1992) suggests that leaders who veer towards being creative and empowering might be 'servant leaders' or possibly social architects who distribute power among community members and facilitate individual and collective development. Duignan and McPherson (1992) argue that it is educative leaders who most successfully promote the interdependence and professional development of colleagues within the constraints of the internal organizational and extra-organizational policies and structures that currently exist. The quality of relationship between middle leaders and teachers that might foster successful self-reflection on and development of practice and help to develop a learning community seem to contain the same elements of authentic relationships that Hopkins *et al.* (1997b) promote for teachers' relationships with their students.

The main criteria that seem to define a learning community, whether in a department or in a whole school, are possibly encapsulated in the following seven indicators but further research is required to establish this:

1. Responsiveness to internal and external policy contexts: middle leaders as mediators and advocates, helping colleagues to come to terms with the contexts in which they work.
2. Emergent facilitative leadership: middle leaders helping teachers and other staff to be involved with principled departmental decisions about the distribution of financial, physical and intellectual resources to take forward learning and teaching effectively, while taking account of the personal and professional interests of staff in particular policy contexts.
3. Evidence of values consensus between department members: a visible and broadly supported coherent vision of the purposes and processes of a department that is constructed by its members and projected by its leader.
4. Evidence of open communications systems, using various formal and informal arenas and channels, through which middle leaders listen to and debate with staff colleagues the development of the department in certain directions generally agreed by its members.
5. Development of practice through consultation within particular policy contexts: middle leaders developing changes in practice through discussion with staff on an explicit basis of educational values and educational perspectives in a department.
6. Development of social cohesion in a collaborative culture that acknowledges the asymmetrical distribution of power that is embedded in hierarchical organizations while recognizing the common humanity and social needs of departmental members.
7. Effective reflexive management: leaders and members improving practice collaboratively through monitoring and evaluating practice in the light of an explicit value base for decision making.

(Busher 2005b)

Creating departmental sub-cultures to develop teaching and learning

The cultures of departments are shaped by middle leaders asserting certain educational, social and epistemological value positions to indicate the social and practice norms to which members of the department are expected to adhere. Other staff members of the department will have some influence over which values are preferred and how they are enacted. But the constructed sub-culture will also affect the actions expected of and by students, too. Sub-cultures of departments are often presented as codes of practice and public morality.

The discussion that follows explores the cultures that were established in a few academic and pastoral departments in secondary schools that were part of a small-scale study carried out by Busher (2002). The middle leaders in this study were said to be effective and worked in schools that regularly took trainee teachers on placements from a university near to them. In these departments codes of practice were clear and often pinned up in classrooms for students and teachers to see. These middle leaders preferred to develop positive interpersonal relationships with staff colleagues and students based on shared values as these helped to construct a sense of community, as Sergiovanni (1992, 2001) expected, which helped to enhance the quality of learning and teaching. This was most clearly demonstrated in one faculty, where professional disagreements between staff appeared not to breach the sense of social cohesion.

> Sometimes we have blazing rows ... over something professional. It is not personal ... But socially as a team, although we are so diverse, we chat in the staff room. At the end of term we have a faculty meal either in school or we go out. Some of the faculty go to the pub on a Friday, not every week ... As a faculty we have a bit of a laugh and a joke ... (female head of faculty)

Middle leaders were closely concerned with the values that were projected through the cultures of their departments, not surprisingly as these profoundly affect the ability of people to work together. The core values they projected were trust of staff and, to a certain extent, students; positively valuing and offering support to colleagues; finding means for engaging staff in dialogue and decision-making; and acknowledging differences between colleagues. Observation of the middle leaders at work as well as interviews with their colleagues supported this view of the values they espoused.

Middle leaders' values for working with staff colleagues emphasized collaborative, rather than collegial cultures:

> Within your subject area it is the team that works together. I have always seen my role within the department as taking a lead in terms of developing schemes of work, of monitoring standards, and discussing ideas within the team. The team contribute to that rather than the leader [being directive]. The subject leader gives suggestions as to what should happen ... maybe draws upon what they have gained from other experiences to bring to the team so the team can share that and have ownership of that. (male head of department)

However, middle leaders acknowledged the unequal distribution of power in their departments, recognizing that they were accountable to their senior staff as well as responsible to their students for what happened in it. 'I act as the lynch pin and also as the person who feeds to the department the aims of the school ... and how we can bring those aims down through into the department and into a classroom level' (female head of faculty).

They regarded themselves as intermediaries between the SMT (senior management team of a school) and their departmental colleagues, both representing their and their colleagues' views to the SMT, as well as acting as agents of the SMT. As the latter, they tried to persuade colleagues to acquiesce to SMT policy, albeit while trying to help colleagues gain ownership of the processes of its implementation.

An important aspect of this collaborative culture was trying to ensure that their departmental colleagues were involved in decision-making, both formally and informally.

> Within the department I would like it run as a sort of cooperative, if you like, where we all make decisions together. Where we take the democratic view that if most people think something is the best way of doing it, that is the way we do it. At times it may come down to me having to say, 'Look, we have got to do this, this way because our hands are tied over certain things.' But ideally my values are that every member of the department has equal worth. (male head of department)

The middle leaders engaged staff in decision-making formally and informally to generate a sense of ownership of departmental policies and practices among staff:

> We have a formal briefing every Thursday morning and then we have a faculty meeting once every four or five weeks on a Monday afternoon after school for an hour. But the actual real running takes place constantly throughout the day, breaks, lunchtimes and during lessons. It is done informally through conversations in here

[department office] ... we wander into each other's lessons without fear of upsetting anyone, and pass on information in that way. (male head of department)

However, to some extent consultation was ritualized in all the formal meetings and through memos that middle leaders passed around, seeking people's views on matters.

Staff were given a positive view of themselves by middle leaders as some of their colleagues acknowledged:

He is very supportive of what we do and tries to give us that sense of our importance in the whole system, and that we are valued. And that is something he does very well and the SMT [before] the new chap [head teacher] came in did not do very well at all. People need to feel valued for what they do. They need to feel when they are not doing it right that they are accountable but none the less valued and supported ... (female teacher)

and supported practically. '[Head of faculty] has this very good knowledge of how things work and who to approach ... the right people to go and talk to and in what order ... She has given me INSET on writing schemes of work' (male teacher).

However, middle leaders also recognized that their colleagues held values, too, as a result of their different work-related life experiences, and they needed to take account of these perspectives when taking decisions in their subject or pastoral area.

People have different backgrounds, different experiences, different expectations of what they want. Often if you are trying to get somewhere, you have all these different people wanting to do it in different directions. I think it is my job to make sure that we are all going in the same direction. I think that is probably the hardest part of my job, managing the different characters in my department. You have to listen to what they are saying, and sometimes it could be about workload, which is a real issue. (female head of faculty)

Teachers' different and sometimes conflicting values are linked to their views of myths and experiences of successful teaching and learning. Sometimes these form the basis of their unwillingness to implement change. Value conflicts may arise at different levels from that of personal preferences to that of cultural imperatives (Hodgkinson 1991). The more that such conflicts are handled at the lowest level, the more likely it is that a compromise can be negotiated.

The cultures that the middle leaders constructed reflected in part who they were as people – their work-related selves – and the social and educational values they had constructed during their lives and careers. These personal attributes affected the relationships they developed with colleagues and students.

> He is a very easy person to work with. He is not demanding. You do what you need to do because you respect him. He is a very approachable man. He will help out if things are going wrong. [He has a good] sense of humour. He is friendly. And you know that he is putting in as much effort as you are. (female teacher)

Another head of department was described as being 'quite benevolent, [but] can be quite dictatorial. She is quite friendly and quite nice as a person. If she gets her teeth into something she won't let go until she has got what she wants with the kids' (male teacher).

They also reflected the views middle leaders held about appropriate ways in which to work with colleagues which sometimes were in conflict with their colleagues' views.

> My own attitudes to people and to life in general were ... I was too easy going, if you like ... a few people thought that ... I should have been more dictatorial in terms of saying to people [when work had to be done] ... that would be a better way of doing things as a leader, not necessarily as a person or as a colleague. (male middle leader)

The collaborative cultures were built on sharing. Middle leaders shared in particular their wide-ranging knowledge of different aspects of their work with their colleagues. They were not just 'nice people'. They offered their colleagues a range of useful resources for surviving in the classroom (the arena of their everyday working lives) from leadership of the subject area in its pedagogy and its organization, to expert knowledge of the workings of the subject, school and education system. For example, one middle leader said, 'Sometimes they will come to me to ask what we are to do next, and I say, well, we are on week 3 and we do this. What I can rely on from them is that if there are any deadlines or any problems, any issues about work they will always keep me informed' (male head of department). This view was corroborated by several of his colleagues.

Teachers in other departments in this study offered similar views of their middle leaders empowering them to be more successful as teachers – 'supporting teachers arranging trips' (female teacher), 'helping teachers learn to plan and file' (male teacher), 'encouraging involvement in external work – examining' (male teacher) – and acting as advocates for them against the dark arts of the schools' senior management team. In addition the middle leaders tried to create for themselves and helped colleagues to create positive working relationships with students.

Middle leaders spent a lot of time and energy undertaking administrative tasks to support the work of their colleagues in their departments, sometimes during lessons when pupils were getting on with their own work, in order to meet deadlines imposed by senior staff or outside sources. This included sorting out other teachers' needs and lesson cover for absent teachers. They spent a lot of their non-contact time visiting colleagues, senior colleagues and administrative offices, and pursuing troublesome students on their own or colleagues' behalf, sometimes to arrange detentions or contact parents.

> So if I am having a problem with one of my students, which I have done, I refer them on to him as subject leader. And then what [he] has done for one of my students was to put him on faculty report and then monitor this student – sent a letter home, spoke to this student after lesson. We have devised a plan for [name of student]. (female teacher)

In doing this, middle leaders seemed to establish a model of servant leadership (Murphy 1992) that cared for and helped others, encouraged their colleagues and students to behave in a similar manner, and created a collaborative culture in their departments that was strongly focused on successful learning and high achievement.

To enhance the sense of community middle leaders tried to encourage colleagues to engage with each other socially to strengthen the merely professional ties of working together as a team.

> Relationships between the faculty are generally very good. We obviously have our spats now and again but overall ... [We] are all fairly young and quite happy to go out and socialize and go to the pub. That tends to have gelled us together. [Male teacher] does not socialize with us so much – we tend to do girlie things – but in terms of the Friday lunch and sitting around chatting, he is there as well. The other members of the faculty in a social sense tend to be alienated, but not so much in a professional sense. (female teacher)

In another department members said that they met occasionally for a quiet meal. Such attempts were not entirely successful, however. In one department the female middle leader admitted:

> The [teachers here] are what we call tired teachers … [leadership] mainly via paper, to be honest … the staff … only work the hours they are required to … They will not stay behind of an evening because we need to have a look at an assessment. That does not happen … That is frustrating.

At the core of these sub-cultures were middle leaders' concerns to deliver high quality learning and teaching to all the students who came to their departments' classes. In part to achieve this they thought they had to perform credibly as teachers themselves, 'not the most innovative but the most effective. You can show that to colleagues through the responses of the students that you teach' (male head of department). Observational data showed that middle leaders used a variety of teaching strategies to differentiate the curriculum and encourage students to engage with learning. Students appeared to spend most of their time on task in well-organized lessons that had clearly defined objectives, sometimes put on a board at the start of a lesson, and suitable resources for the intended variety of activities.

Middle leaders explained the sort of culture they tried to establish with their students and encouraged their colleagues in their departments to establish, too.

> We want to give them an appreciation of the subject. We want them to fulfil their potential. We want them to go as far as they can to be critically aware, and to appreciate the subject even if they don't continue with it … I have always believed that there should be a certain joy from learning and an enthusiasm from learning because it is not just a subject that you teach. (male middle leader)

They wanted students to have a sense of achievement, whatever assessment grades they gained, by 'encouraging students to develop their strengths and build on that … acknowledging students as individuals and then identifying those areas. Students certainly see [exam success] as important themselves … but I think it is something about how they can stretch themselves individually, rather than [just] being focused on [grades]' (female middle leader). They also wanted them to have a sense that their teachers cared for them and respected them. To achieve this, subject leaders worked closely with colleagues in preparing schemes of work, providing the resources to sustain that, and applying regimes of assessment to monitor student performance.

However, these departments were not isolated oases but firmly embedded in the socio-political contexts of school policy and of wider national educational policy. Middle leaders were painfully aware of how these affected their work with colleagues and helped colleagues to be aware of these too. Not only the National Curriculum limited the scope of their choices about teaching and learning – 'I would quite happily [only] talk about rainforests, coasts and rivers … but the National Curriculum also says I have to do settlement, population, development' (female subject leader) – but management processes for schools imposed by central government affected the sub-cultures of their departments too. 'Quite a lot of people are not very happy about doing performance management but recognize that … it is a hoop that they have to jump through' (female subject leader).

Middle leaders also asserted that their relationships with colleagues and students was affected by the local communities in which their schools were located. 'The main problem is [students saying] 'I am not part of this religion. My dad says I don't have to do this. So I am not going to learn it' … I don't know what sort of programmes they watch at home' (male subject leader).

The distribution of power and the hierarchy of authority in schools, especially the legitimacy of the senior management team (SMT) to manage the school strategically, also affected the sub-cultures of their departments. 'Basically the school will lay out what areas they want covered on the school improvement plan … I will have six sections to fill in with the headings laid down by SMT and then we will have a humanities section' (female subject leader). Consequently middle leaders could at best only establish collaborative rather than collegial sub-cultures in their departments.

Commentary

The central work of leaders, especially leaders of departments or subjects in secondary schools is to create a culture that they signal through the interpersonal relationships that they develop with their colleagues. A key element in this development is the social and educational values that middle leaders hold and which underpin the cultures they create.

These cultures are manifested in various ways and became symbols of collective identity. The sub-cultures gave the departments identities which bound their leaders equally with the other members in establishing the norms and practices of each department (group or community), which Schein (1992) argued was the function of organizational cultures or sub-cultures. The cultures created by these middle leaders in these departments in this study seem to have been quasi-collegial sub-cultures of the sort recommend by Hopkins (2001) as being necessary for improving schooling in England. However, the hierarchical relationships between middle leaders and teachers was always visible and openly acknowledged by teachers and middle leaders.

No claim is made that all middle leaders establish such cultures, indeed it is expected that other leaders in other schools and departments might create different cultures and sub-cultures which would have different impacts on the ways in which teachers work together and work with students and their parents and with senior staff. Although it is possible to map the cultures created by leaders with the help or despite the resistance of their colleagues, the explanations of those cultures and the norms, values and beliefs they encapsulate will depend in part on the individual people who form a department, what they perceive to be their needs, interests and values educationally and socially, and how they perceive those needs being supported or denied by the values, beliefs, practices and policies manifested and developed by their leaders, in this case the middle leaders of subject and pastoral department teams.

9 Strategies of success at middle leader level

Focusing on middle leaders

Micro-politics lies at the interface between agency and social structure (Ball 1987), describing the ways in which actors engage with the social systems and structures (Giddens 1984) that surround them. As such, understanding them is fundamental to understanding not only the leadership of schools (Hoyle 1986) but also the resistance that people encounter when trying to implement policies and practices. Micro-political processes, then, describe holistically all the interactions of people in organizations (Ball 1987), allowing educational organizations and communities (Sergiovanni 1994) to be viewed as political systems in which participants are political actors with their own interests and values. Educational decision-making and practice from whole-school to classroom level is the primary arena of conflict and negotiation (Bacharach 1983).

Actors in schools (staff, students and parents) and the stakeholders outside school engage with the policies that emerge in different national and local arenas in society, and internally through the actions of managers at various levels in a school's hierarchy (although primarily from senior staff), through a variety of different micro-political strategies. Through these they try to project power to shape decisions to promote their own preferred values. Their actions are purposeful if not always overtly explained. As social systems are made up of individuals (Greenfield 1993), what is being described is how actors engage with other actors singly and in groups, some of whom have more power than others through access to a variety of different types of resources. As each actor's different personality or personhood (Aubrey et al. 2000) is part of the process of social interaction, this, too, is a source of power that varies in strength from one person to another. Weber (1947) described this as charisma.

One such group of actors in secondary schools is the middle leaders. These include subject leaders, who are sometimes called heads of department – indicating their position in the school organizational hierarchy – and pastoral leaders, and cross-curriculum leaders. The category should also include managers of services, too, such as site supervisors and senior clerical staff (Busher and Saran 1995). These post-holders are said to be at the heart of efforts to improve the quality of teaching and learning in schools (Hopkins *et al.* 1994; Harris 1999). Especially in larger schools, it is they who lead the implementation of subject-related and pastoral policies as well as the transformation of the policies of senior management and those required by central government into practices that can be implemented successfully in the 'classroom' – a term used loosely here to refer to any organized arena in which learning is intended to take place.

Middle leaders coordinate the work of staff and students in various types of pastoral and academic departments (organizational sub-units) in secondary schools in England and Wales. They are people who inhabit and rule the middle realm (Siskin 1994) of the organizational hierarchy of schools. Blase and Anderson (1995) describe leadership as a use of power over, with or through other people. Middle leaders offer leadership to their colleagues and students through using a range of social, symbolic and material resources as sources of power and authority to try to shape their colleagues' actions – Giddens (1984) talks about this as controlling other people's actions. Values emerge through the use of these sources of power as certain principles and practices were privileged over others.

Locating middle leaders in their educational organizational frameworks

Middle leaders, as Bennett *et al.* (2003) point out, hold a diverse range of posts including those of heads of subject department and pastoral leaders. The functions that middle leaders are expected to carry out by senior staff, staff colleagues, students and parents, and how they are expected to enact these, are framed and limited by the cultures, traditions and histories around them of the institutions within which they find themselves (Foucault 1986) and by those other people (students and parents as well as support staff, academic colleagues and senior staff) with whom they work. A recent study by Bennett *et al.* (2003) outlines these in some detail, elaborating views put forward by the Teacher Training agency (TTA 1998) which are shown in Figure 9.1 (page 135). In carrying out their functions, middle leaders have to engage with the social, macro-political and organizational systems that surround them, in part to mediate the policies and pressures that arise from these to other teachers and students in their departments. Reay (1998) points out how the micro-political processes of teachers trace their struggle against control from central government (and she might have

Figure 9.1 Four task areas for subject leaders

a   providing strategic direction and subject development – subject area as knowledge framework (Siskin 1994); bridging and brokering with internal school aspects of departmental context (Glover *et al.* 1998), e.g. negotiating with senior staff; negotiating with other departments – advocacy (Bradley and Roaf 1995); acting as a successful role model

b   improving teaching and learning – pedagogy; SEN inclusivity; being a role model; appraisal and performance management (DfEE 1998); overseeing assessment and curriculum; evaluating value-added figures for a subject area

c   leading and managing staff – the importance of creating a particular culture/social cohesion (Hargreaves 1994; Hopkins 2001; McGregor 2000); communicating with staff informally and formally in different arenas of negotiation/space, a social and physical construction (Little 1993); negotiating with staff in own subject area (Busher 2001)

d   effective deployment of staff and resources – staff development (Harris 1999); appraisal and performance management (see above); but also (Simkins 1997) resource allocation as a value-laden activity.

(source: TTA 1998; additional references show some links to related research in education)

added from senior staff in schools, too) while searching for autonomy to pursue in practice their own constructed educational values.

Where these functions are defined by senior staff, middle leaders are usually delegated authority, a form of power, to carry these out. In so doing, senior staff make accessible certain sources of power to middle leaders to use if and when they choose. There is a major debate at present about whether such delegation of power constitutes distributed leadership (Gronn 2003) or whether that notion represents a different quality altogether. The range of the functions of middle leaders is problematic. Busher *et al.* (2000), drawing on the work of Glover *et al.* (1998) among others, as well as on their own research, argue that there are three other functions that middle managers carry out in addition to those developed by the TTA. These are:

1. Creating professional networks: liaising with LEA, public examination bodies; subject associations; professional associations.
2. Liaising with local external contexts of school, including parents.
3. Exerting power and influences – related to resources (including financial and symbolic); taking decisions; acting as a successful role model; being personally successful at work.

Middle leaders have to engage with the social and organizational contexts that surround them, in part to mediate the policies and pressures that arise from these to the other teachers and students in their departments. The policy contexts faced by middle managers can be divided into the external and internal policy contexts of a school. The external ones occur at national, local or regional and, for departments in schools, institutional levels. The national level includes, in England, central government policed frameworks such as the National Curriculum, OFSTED inspections, Key Stage 3 strategies and the introduction of performance management into schools. They also include other influential curriculum frameworks policed by public examination boards which are regulated by central government.

At local or regional level (Riley *et al.* 2000; Busher and Barker 2003), external policy contexts include the impact of local government policies and those communities from which schools' students come on how staff, students and parents engage with each other and with the curriculum. Other elements in the local contexts of a school influence the teaching strategies that middle leaders and their colleagues can employ as well as disciplinary ones. These include the social composition of the population of a school's catchment area (Thrupp 1999; Wells 1996); the competition from other local schools for students, especially those who are more able academically (Edwards *et al.* 1989), as well as the competence of its local education authority (Busher and Barker 2003). For example, it is difficult to run after-school clubs or detentions when many students travel to school by bus, as they do in many rural areas, and these buses leave within a few minutes of the ending of the school day.

The internal policy contexts, the micro-sphere of the school, for middle leaders are constructed and projected by a school's senior management team (Grace 1995). Schools are construed as sites of policy processes (Grace 1995; Bowe *et al.* 1992) which are sustained by asymmetrical and negotiable relationships of power between school members. In these institutions organizational structures are no more, though no less, than the historical outcomes of negotiative processes, the reflections of past and present hierarchical relationships within the school that are sustained and eroded by changing socio-political contexts as projected through the agency of participants in them, especially those who are more powerful. Like leaders at all levels in a school, middle managers mediate the values and demands from these contexts to their colleagues, their students and their students' parents and carers. However, these participants also form a context in which middle leaders take decisions to make teaching and learning relevant to and appropriately differentiated for every student. Values lie at the heart of the purposeful actions of middle leaders as actors as they try to pursue the educational interests of their students and the work-related and occasionally personal interests of their colleagues and, more rarely, of themselves.

Sustaining community norms: endorsing the power of the collective

To sustain and improve successful teaching and learning, middle leaders have to create socially cohesive departments because these help colleagues to work together successfully, and help students to receive the best teaching and learning opportunities possible in the school organizational framework and the social catchment area that it serves. Middle leaders do not perceive this as an easy task. How middle leaders carry out this task and the other functions shown in Table 9.1 depends on the social and educational values and beliefs they hold, their knowledge of the epistemology of their subject or pastoral area, the cultures they help to create in their subject areas, the policies they negotiate to enact these functions, the repertoire of skills and knowledge they have for managing departments, the skill with which they access and apply a variety of sources of power to create and enact policy, the repertoire of micro-political strategies they understand and deploy appropriately to negotiate with departmental colleagues and senior staff and implement policy and practice.

Table 9.1 Expectations of middle leaders' work by senior staff and colleagues

Formally ascribed by senior staff	Examples
Working with recalcitrant students	We have a table outside the door [of my classroom] so people will put kids out there … and I have to go and sort them out … Because I am their [teacher's] next step up and knowing staff as I do, I know which kids I need to go out to and sort out. (female head of geography)
Supporting subject colleagues	I am there in terms of discipline, in terms of advice, in terms of providing assessments, instructions and so on. To make sure that it is all supportive, and that they do feel confident … [and] happy … [so] you will teach better and then you will get better results. (female head of geography)
Supervising the work of subject colleagues	It is the subject leader's responsibility to make sure that the teachers in his or her department are producing the goods … in the classroom and the paperwork, and what the hierarchy needs, and what the LEA or government requires. If you know that your staff are doing it anyway, then that makes the job a lot easier. (male head of English)

cont.

Formally ascribed by senior staff	Examples
Managing the subject area and providing material resources	There is the admin., the exam entries, the mocks [exams] ... doing the filing and buying the books ... the creativity of making up schemes [of work] ... Having the chance to have a budget, plan it, implement it and see it actually happening. (male head of RE) Making sure adequate resources are available for teaching.
Providing expert knowledge	I have always seen my role ... as taking a lead ... in developing schemes of work, of monitoring standards, and discussing ideas within the team ... The subject leader gives suggestions ... maybe draws upon what they have gained from other experiences to bring to the team. (male head of history)
Mediating senior staff policy to departmental colleagues	In terms of implementing [senior management policy] ... If we are given something we need to implement ... [we] would sit down and discuss ... the implications that had, and we would try and think through the problems before we presented it [to the humanities faculty]. (female head of humanities)
Having a vision for the subject area	To know where the department is going, to have the vision for where the department is to be in one year, in two years, in five years. (female head of humanities)
Effective planning	It is my job to work with the department in setting targets for that ... but then to work with them and take on board their ideas as how to move the department on. (female head of humanities) Being a good strategic planner and leader of things. (female history teacher) Ensuring that targets are clear for students. (female history teacher) Monitoring student progress through assessment and reporting.

Informally ascribed by senior staff	Examples
Helping subject area colleagues understand the school system	[She] has this very good knowledge of how things work and who to approach ... She seems to know protocol very well ... for organizing trips ... the right people to go and talk to and in what order ... She has helped me write application letters. (male humanities teacher)

cont.

Informally ascribed by senior staff	Examples
Advocacy: promoting the interests of the subject area	I had some trouble with [a] trip … with the senior management after I had been [site] and looked round and done the worksheets, and senior management suddenly said we couldn't go. [Head of Faculty] was straight up [to them]: 'Why? This is what [I] ha[d] done [already], taken one day out of her half term to go there. We have booked the coach, sent out letters [to parents], so why are you now preventing it going? (female RE teacher)
Creating a collaborative culture	The importance of trust between colleagues, as well as between teachers and students, is complemented by the importance of fairness and justice. (female history teacher) Keeping staff informed and reminding them of deadlines. Listening to staff views.

Note: The quotations are drawn from interviews that formed part of a study of middle leaders (Busher 2002)

Constructing a socially cohesive sub-culture in their departments offers middle leaders a source of power for implementing their policies in keeping with the news of Lenski (1986). The more closely middle leaders address the work-related and personal needs of their colleagues, the more they encourage colleagues to consent to their leadership, i.e. use transformational approaches to leadership, the stronger is the consent and support they are likely to gain from colleagues for their policies because colleagues think they have part ownership of them. Further participants welcome being members of such cultures or sub-cultures because they think it furthers their work (Busher 2002). Students appear to respond positively to it too. This culture is discussed more fully in Chapter 8.

Negotiating with senior staff is problematic. Acting as advocates (Bradley and Roaf 1995) does not simply involve middle leaders conveying information to senior staff, but sometimes going to senior staff to persuade them to change their minds about policies that they were threatening to introduce. Middle leaders act in this way when they and/or their colleagues think agreed subject area values and policies are under threat from senior staff actions. A key strategy of successful advocacy is showing how a department's proposed actions fit closely with the core values of the school, meet its interests by being carefully planned and managed, and bring esteem in some way to a school.

This is not a toothless advocacy since middle leaders have the power of the collective department to support them. For example, some middle leaders tried to help their subject area colleagues gain some control of the processes of policy implementation (Busher 2002). From this base, the middle leaders were able to enter into negotiations with senior staff and modify the implementation of practice, though not the policy itself. Sometimes middle leaders can build alliances with other people or departments in the school or outside it to exert pressure on senior staff. It generates a sort of countervailing power to that of the senior staff. Middle leaders in the study by Busher (2002) developed alliances with school governors and drew on reports by OFSTED inspectors to press home their cases. In an earlier study (Busher 1992) middle leaders talked of alliances with LEA advisers and local universities as means of trying to exert power over senior staff decisions.

Leaders have many strategies for constructing a socially cohesive department, that can be loosely collected into a variety of 'styles' of leadership, as is illustrated in Figure 9.2. But leaders at all levels in a school might use any of these strategies to at some time or another help staff and students to engage in learning successfully.

Figure 9.2 A typology for leadership

Servant leader
Leaders who lead from the nexus of a web of interpersonal relationships, not from the apex of a hierarchy, to empower teachers and release their creative abilities. Professional expertise, not line authority, is their base of influence.

Organizational architect
Leaders who create flatter organizational structures creating a greater sense of ownership by teachers and a more committed workforce.

Moral educator
Leaders show deep personal values and beliefs – showing ethic of care for all by putting people first, valuing and responding to the unique needs of each member of their department.

Social architect
Leaders who design and construct social networks to address the social and economic conditions facing staff and students; develop partnerships with parents and communities outside the school; sensitive to racial, cultural and gender issues.

Leading professional
c.f. Hughes (1985) teachers as extended professionals. Leaders need expertise in pedagogy, organizing departments and liaising with people and be more than competent as teachers.

Note: the first four categories are taken from Murphy (1992)

(source: Brown 1996)

Whatever strategies are used, successful middle leaders seem to try to preserve key values of high standards of work and performance by students and teachers, coupled with a care for people's needs and difficulties and a belief that students should have the best education possible that is suitable to them (Busher 1992, 2002).

Supporting and supervising staff: enhancing capacity

An important element in middle leaders' success in running departments is their ability to help colleagues develop their capacities as teachers and leaders. To do this, leaders need to understand colleagues' personal and work-related needs and interests and help them to understand the culture of their particular school, to engage with the sub-culture of the department and to appreciate the complexity of students' small cultures (Holliday 2005). One of the major blockages to change is the difficulties of matching up the needs and work-related values and attitudes of individual staff and students with the needs of the school or department as an organization. Hall (1997: 152) suggests that the most effective processes of staff development recognize that 'there is an overlap between education's central purpose and the meaning of work to those working in education. [Thus] there is greater scope for synchronicity of individual and school needs than exists in, for example, banking or manufacturing ... The creative leader recognizes and works with this commitment within a collaborative rather than a conflict approach which drives people apart.'

There are several different approaches to staff development that can be pursued by middle leaders, all of which may be more or less appropriate in particular circumstances. Lomax (1990) lists four of these:

1. A research perspective which might be described also as an extended professional (*sic*) approach since it requires teachers to consider their practice in their national, institutional and personal professional (*sic*) contexts.
2. A political/micro-political perspective which defines staff development in terms of how it can meet national, local and institutional agenda regardless of the actual relevance of particular developments to teachers' support for learners, e.g. ensuring that all teachers are computer literate because it is government policy even though such skills are rarely used in classrooms when there are insufficient computers in schools.
3. A management/administrative approach which emphasizes the importance of a school's corporate goals and of its institutional/ bureaucratic needs, e.g. considerable expenditure on training staff in administering records of achievement or in marking attendance

registers. The five training days for teachers in England and Wales available under the Teachers Pay and Conditions Act (1987) were intended to focus in this way on whole school needs rather than on individual staff or department needs.

4. A restricted approach that only focuses on working with children in classrooms.

The first offers middle leaders the greatest opportunities for empowering colleagues to become proactive learners and help build a learning community. However, for certain limited circumstances the management approach can offer a means of developing technical skills with colleagues (support staff as well as teachers), as long as staff have collaborated with the middle leader in identifying the needs for such training. It may also be appropriate in circumstances where teachers, as a result of appraisal, have identified the need to enhance their pedagogical knowledge and skills further but are unwilling to engage in a research approach.

To sustain a socially cohesive departmental community, middle leaders need to engage staff in approaches to staff development that facilitate their engagement with educational values and departmental policy-making, as well as technical instrumental aspects of teaching, learning and assessment. McGill and Beaty (2001) suggest that action learning helps to do this, in ways similar to that propounded for action research (Somekh 2000) or teacher-led curriculum development (Frost and Durrant 2003). They discuss how participants can work together to offer each other collaborative support. This constructs staff as co-creators of a community or sub-community's (department's, for example) policy and practice, emphasizing their co-ownership of their own and their community's development. Action learning focuses on real problems in an organization for which individuals have responsibility. To help understand and resolve problems, people join together in groups (or action learning sets) to share ideas with each other, to analyse situations and then develop various strategies to resolve them. Although the members of the group learn from each other, individual members are left with their responsibilities intact for implementing the chosen solutions to the identified problems. Hopkins *et al.* (1997b) talk of a similar process that they call 'pedagogic partnerships', groups of teachers working together inside and outside the classroom to bring about improvement in teaching and learning.

Such approaches can be complemented by more formal means of staff development, such as mentoring (Moyles *et al.* 1998). It is a mistake to think that the notion of mentoring only applies to the induction of new entrants into the teaching profession whether as initial trainees or as newly qualified teachers. It is a role and process that can be used by any member of staff to help others modify their practice, although it is usually carried out by more experienced staff acting as critical friends to less experienced colleagues. Moyles *et al.* (1998) suggest that, as well as mentors needing to be flexible in their style of working with staff, they need to be able to use a wide range of skills:

- flexible in their style of working with staff
- use a wide range of interpersonal skills effectively
- effective communication
- sound professional practice
- sound professional knowledge involving a wide range of pedagogic and analytical skills
- negotiative and enabling skills
- fostering self-esteem
- patience.

They use these skills to carry out six main functions:

- Professional supporter – who encourages and reassures their colleagues in their actions.
- Professional trainer – who coaches colleagues and helps them to clarify what situations need.
- Professional educator – to encourage colleagues to reflect critically, on the basis of evidence, on their actions.
- Professional assessor – to offer an evaluation of performance according to agreed criteria.
- Professional sponsor – able to help colleagues negotiate the organizational structures.
- Personal friend and counsellor.

Helping staff to develop their practice has to begin with helping them to evaluate their practice, whether through processes of action research or through processes of appraisal. Either way, a first step to bringing about change in their practices is to consider the environments within which they are working:

- identifying what changes are needed and what are the environmental constraints and supports for that change
- identifying the needs of individuals involved in the changes and seeing how individual and organizational needs can be meshed together creatively
- finding ways of getting colleagues engaged
- identifying what practices to implement to bring about change
- planning and resourcing and helping people to engage with processes of change within an agreed time frame
- monitoring and evaluating the processes and outcomes of change.

There are two main perspectives for evaluating staff practice or helping staff to evaluate their own practices. The first emphasizes a hierarchical approach of judgement where more senior staff use their authority of office to evaluate the work of others. The second emphasizes a more collaborative approach where the agenda for carrying out the review of practice may be held jointly by appraiser and appraisee or just by the appraisee. However, both require effective observation of practice; sensitive interaction between staff and supporter/mentor/appraiser; successful feedback or debriefing after observation; the setting of agreed targets for staff to undertake as an outcome of discussions between them and the appraiser; an identification of any further work-related education that may be needed. Randell *et al.* (1990) suggest that the purposes of appraisal are as follows:

- Evaluation – to enable an organization to share out 'fairly' (*sic*) the money, promotion and prerequisites available.
- Auditing – to discover the work potential, both present and future of individuals and departments.
- Constructing succession plans – for manpower (*sic*), department and corporate planning.
- Discovering training needs – by exposing inadequacies and deficiencies that could be remedied by training.
- Motivating staff – to reach organizational standards and objectives.
- Developing individuals – by advice, information and attempts at shaping their behaviour by praise or punishment.
- Checking – the effectiveness of personnel procedures and practices.

Constructing the future through working positively with people

Being a successful leader or middle leader is synonymous with being an astute politician within an institution who understands: how organizational systems work; the range of values and interests that individual people hold; the checks and balances influencing policy creation and projection; the construction of pressure groups and cohesive coalitions, and how power can be used to implement policies to sustain and transform departments in educational institutions. Middle leaders can access some sources of power because of their rank in the hierarchy of the school organization. These include access to: delegated authority, systemic resources, material resources and various aspects of the socio-economic, political and epistemological contexts of their work. Other sources of power can be accessed through their work-related and personal knowledge. This is discussed more fully in Chapter 3. Middle leaders exercise power to enact their own and other people's – usually senior staff – policy. When pushed they admit they occasionally use their authority to command (coerce) people into acting in certain ways (Busher 2002), but seem to prefer to use their influence through persuasion, inviting colleagues to share in a negotiated vision for their department by acting in particular ways.

Middle leaders use a range of micro-political strategies to construct and implement policy and practice, some of which might be classified as coercive transactional strategies, while others might be considered to be collegial transformational strategies. Central to their success is the creation of a purposeful culture, encompassing a vision for the future that is at least professionally collaborative among staff but also encourages the building of social networks, too, where colleagues want them. In departments and epistemic communities where this occurs there appears to develop communities of practice focused on developing teaching and learning that are more socially cohesive than the formal contractual basis of educational organizations might lead an observer to expect (Busher 1992, 2002). This appears to uphold the contention of various authors (e.g. Hopkins 2001; Fullan 2001) that transformational leadership is essential for bringing about improvement in schools.

The micro-political strategies used by middle leaders in various arenas in schools to achieve their agenda can be subdivided into three categories. The first is strategies that are available from the authority delegated to them as distributed leaders by senior staff. These might be summarized as follows:

- offering systemic resources to sustain colleagues; use of authority to support colleagues and acting as an advocate for the team with senior staff, students and parents
- offering material resources to help colleagues and to project their vision of effective teaching, learning and departmental organization through helping to sustain and transform the curriculum by the creation and application of physical and financial resources.

The second category is those strategies that arise from a leader's person. These might take the form of offering social resources:

- making the department a pleasant place in which to work; enhancing social cohesion
- organizing the subject or pastoral area to emphasize team work and collaboration
- negotiating carefully with other people and showing care of them and for them
- being approachable and developing trust with colleagues and students.

The third arises from a leader's work-related knowledge and skills. These might include:

- offering symbolic resources, such as a vision for the subject area which incorporates core values for staff and students, which privileges some actions and not others, as well as how the department fits into school plans for development; projecting a coherent set of educational and social values
- offering organizational resources: the knowledge that middle leaders have of how systems work and people work in organizational systems; of students and how to work with them
- offering technical knowledge of curriculum subjects; of subject pedagogy; being an effective teacher.

The second and third categories are accessible to anybody in an institution, including students in schools, as a means of manifesting their agency.

What leads to middle leaders' success or failure in the maintenance or development of policy and practice is how skilfully they use their repertoire of micro-political strategies to project their leadership by drawing in complex ways on a variety of sources of power. This allows them to work in the values-led contingency manner that Day et al. (2000) found among successful head teachers and suggest help to create an improving school. Many of the criteria proposed by Stoll and Fink (1998) for healthy cultures in schools applied to the departments in the study by Busher (2002). The sub-cultures of those departments could have been described as collegial but for the persistence of stubbornly asymmetrical power relationships between middle leaders and their departmental colleagues, as they and their colleagues acknowledged, that raise questions about the nature of collegiality and the nature of democratic leadership (Woods et al. 2003) in institutions that are fundamentally hierarchical.

Middle leaders' concern to present themselves as the first among equals in their departments and preserve collaborative approaches to working with their colleagues indicates their awareness of the power of the collective (Lukes 1974). It acts as a restraint on middle leaders in developing and implementing policy and leads to them, where possible, negotiating compromises, for example between senior staff policies that they are expected to implement in their departments and modes of implementation that departmental colleagues find acceptable. Middle leaders' unwillingness to coerce colleagues into acting in particular ways (Busher 2002) acknowledges, tacitly, the importance of having their colleagues' consent for their policies if these and their leadership are to be sustained successfully, even though they are appointed to their offices by senior staff. This fits with the view of Lenski (1986) that ruling elites construct rules to legitimate certain actions and processes in communities because the repeated use of coercion is costly and corrosive of social cohesion. Middle leaders used similar strategies with students in these schools (Busher 2002), grounding the legitimacy of their demands and actions on appeals to internal school rules or external demands, such as public examination timetables, on schools and students.

In most observed debates between teachers and middle leaders in departments the focus was on work-related policy – what values were being implemented in whose interests and who should do what and with what resources (Busher 2002). People contested proposed policy and changes to practice from their own work-related and personal interests or perspectives. There were no teachers in these departments who did not engage in these debates whether informally over coffee or in formally constructed meetings. Action as much as speech was a means of engagement through which non-promoted colleagues also exercised power. For example, some teachers indicated their views on policy and practice by using a strategy of slowly implementing agreed departmental policy – not completing student assessment forms on time; failing to return textbooks (let alone tidily) to a stock cupboard after lessons – thereby inconveniencing their colleagues. Middle leaders made use of their formal authority to press forward their views on these and other matters, but also drew on their negotiative skills and informal influence to help colleagues to join in with the policies they were proposing or implementing.

Throughout these debates and negotiations, whether in formal (e.g. classroom, staff room) or informal (e.g. corridors) arenas, power flowed as people struggled to assert their values in particular situations. Power became visible as middle leaders bartered and built visions of success with their colleagues (and students, too), asking them to enact certain policies in exchange for being able to shape the ways in which the policies were implemented, finding the touchstone of people's work-related values and interests which would allow them to support that policy, even if grudgingly, rather than resist it. These middle leaders seem to have been successful as much because they were astute politicians as because of the technical knowledge they had, their particular personal skills, or the authority of office they had been given.

10 Leading purposeful change in schools:
People, power and culture

Developing school communities to promote student engagement

To make sense of change processes, let alone to enact them successfully, teachers need an understanding of modernist systems perspectives as well as of critical perspectives that explain how people negotiate with each other to implement particular agenda or developments and why some people are marginalized in these discussions. Lukes (1986) notes that understanding how power flows in organizations makes it possible for people to be manipulative of others – projecting power through others rather than using it with them – but it also allows people altruistically to alter systems and process to minimize the marginalization of some groups of people, such as school students from ethnic minority groups in some schools. However, bringing about change successfully also requires participants to understand the cultures of communities in which they are trying to enact change, so they appreciate how the norms and beliefs of those communities can support or hinder change. So change involves leaders and their colleagues creating, organizing, managing, monitoring and resolving the value conflicts inherent in change processes, where values are defined as concepts of the desirable (Hodgkinson 1999) that are used to construct utopian visions (Halpin 2003) to guide practice. It is this political cultural and axiological debate that lies at the heart of developing inclusive schooling.

In the first section of this chapter modernist or systems perspectives on school improvement are interlaced with critical perspectives to make visible the dynamics of managing changes. Change comes about because people espouse and pursue particular agenda and access power in various ways to try to implement them either within existing social (organizational) structures or by changing these or the rules through which these are constructed (Giddens 1984). These agenda are value laden and raise questions about what values should be implemented through schooling and whose interests the change seekers are trying to serve.

The second section of the chapter focuses on the issue of values that might lead to socially just and, therefore, engaging schooling for all students. It asserts that schooling should be based on these values to help students to develop their social capital so that they can aspire to take whatever opportunities are available to them in national or local adult society. It considers how teachers might begin to map and implement an agenda for social justice in schools in order to create genuinely inclusive education that cares and caters equitably for vulnerable, marginalized and challenging students along with those students who already engage successfully with schooling.

The discussion of modernist or systems perspectives is focused on school improvement. The term 'school improvement' is problematic because, first, it assumes that things are always getting better. However, change and development may not benefit all groups in a school equally or indeed at all, and arguably if the implementation of change requires scarce resources it is likely to lead to some groups which are not at the focus of the change being worse off, if only temporarily, even if it is only because teachers spend more time on developing the changes and less time on working with particular groups of students. Second, notions of improvement are culturally located, so what is considered 'improvement' in one culture (and one time and space in history) may not be so considered in another. As there is no absolute definition of what constitutes 'better', whether or not there is improvement will depend on people's value-laden perspectives. For example, in England and Wales in the twentieth century there was a strong move in schools to include boys and girls in the same classes, whatever the age of the boys and girls. Some parents resisted but most parents welcomed this, not least because it seemed to expand the educational opportunities available to girls (women). However, in some parts of the world and among some faith groups in Britain such developments are not considered improvements at all, rather as a threat to established cultures.

This challenges the notion, often asserted by people promoting school improvement, that there is one model for bringing about change that can be used in all places regardless of the cultures in those places. Instead it suggests that processes for bringing about change and development have to be culturally relevant to the sites in which they are being enacted. So it is important to be clear from where particular ideas come and what cultural assumptions are implicit in them before they can be considered suitable for adoption or adaptation at another site.

The underlying five principles of school improvement are said to be:

1. Enhancing the quality of students' learning.
2. The vision of the school should embrace all members of the school community as learners and contributors.

3. External pressures for change are perceived as important opportunities for a school to secure its internal priorities.
4. Schools seek to develop structures and create conditions that encourage collaboration and lead to empowerment of individuals and groups.
5. Schools promote the view that monitoring and evaluating quality is a responsibility that all members of staff share.

(Hopkins *et al.* 1997a: 1)

These principles aim to re-develop the capacity of teachers to evaluate and enhance the quality of learning and teaching in their particular social, educational and organizational contexts, as Fullan (2001) argues, and convert the fragmented and competition-oriented organizational cultures that were encouraged in schools in England and Wales in the 1980s and 1990s back towards collaborative if not collegial ones. The focus on implementing effective teaching and learning strategies and the emphasis on 'all students' points in the direction of inclusive education policies is equally crucial since these are the core processes of the school. But these have to be facilitated by leaders in schools shaping policies, practices and cultures in particular ways. Hopkins (2001) emphasizes the importance of leadership that is largely transformational and focuses on the instructional processes of a school, facilitating effective collaborative working between members of a school (teachers, students, parents and governors).

MacGilchrist *et al.* (2004: 113) develop this into a series of nine intelligences that leaders at any level in a school need to develop with their colleagues and students and their parents:

1. *Ethical intelligence* – justice; respect for persons; inclusion; rights and responsibilities.
2. *Spiritual intelligence* – search for meaning; transcendancy; sense of community; interconnectedness.
3. *Contextual intelligence* – internal; local; national; global.
4. *Operational intelligence* – strategic thinking; development planning; management arrangements; distributed leadership.
5. *Emotional intelligence* – self-awareness; awareness of others; managing emotions; developing emotional literacy.
6. *Collegial intelligence* – commitment to shared purpose; knowledge creation; multi-level learning; trust and curiosity.
7. *Reflective intelligence* – creating time for reflection; self-evaluation; deep learning; feedback for learning.
8. *Pedagogical intelligence* – new visions and goals for learning; teaching for learning; open classrooms; going against the grain.
9. *Systematic intelligence* – mental models; systems thinking; self-organization; networking.

One particular programme for school improvement, IQEA (Improving the Quality of Education for All), grounds school development in teachers creating, in a structured way, a rational and well-researched approach to change that will reduce functional barriers to effective teaching and learning and diminish cultural barriers, too (Hopkins and Reynolds 2001). To coordinate an IQEA project, a school is expected to set up a temporary or task-related organizational structure called a school improvement group (SIG) or cadre which is led by a school's IQEA coordinator, who may or may not be a member of the school's senior staff. The cadre is a steering group of normally six to ten people, composed of a range of staff of different status and curriculum expertise. It is responsible for administering the 'conditions' surveys at the start of a school's involvement with IQEA – which provides a base-line view of the culture of the school from the perspectives of students and staff when it starts its project – and conveying their analyses to staff. These are used to focus a school's development goal and the key steps to achieve it. It is also responsible for developing a strategy of professional development to support teachers constructing and implementing these steps and, later, holding a cross-curriculum workshop where teachers can compare and celebrate their developments (West 2000). However, in the evaluation of IQEA in a large shire local authority in England it was clear that such developments did not work successfully unless they had the support of the school leaders. In other words, for change to be enacted successfully, power has to be used appropriately (Watling *et al.* 2003).

Hopkins (2001) suggested IQEA works because it:

- encourages the questioning of existing practice
- supports a collegiate approach – the cadre
- focuses improvement on the classroom but also acknowledges the need to work on conditions in school – staff development, leadership, planning, etc.
- stimulates ideas
- focuses on the main processes of schools – teaching and learning
- transforms the culture of the school into one that is positive in respecting people and celebrating learning.

This view implicitly asserts the importance of teachers being empowered to take a proactive part in bringing about change in their schools. In allowing teachers to gain a share in the ownership of change, this process encourages them to engage with it because it allows them to implement some of their values for constructing successful learning and teaching to benefit their students. Further, it offers them a range of resources to bring this about, including time for staff development, material resources for curriculum and staff development, and knowledge resources, especially from the teams running IQEA, to help them develop and evaluate relevant changes in pedagogy.

To foster such approaches to change, leaders at whatever level in an organization need to offer their colleagues instrumental and cultural help. Morgan (1986) suggests they have particular functions to perform among their colleagues such as:

- looking ahead for policy and technology changes, and to assess the strengths and weaknesses of their own organizations or departments compared with others
- identifying problems and opportunities
- finding ways of reframing problems so the negatives become potential positives – new avenues for development
- grasping, shaping and developing these opportunities to implementation.

Fullan and Hargreaves (1992: 112) argue that leaders need to understand the social contexts of change for their colleagues individually and collectively and mediate these to them. They suggest that leaders should:

- understand the culture
- value teachers: promote their professional growth (find something to value and praise in each teacher's work)
- extend what they value (breadth of vision that is inclusive of all good practice, not just including a leader's preferences)
- express what they value (remember the importance of using symbols to reflect values)
- promote collaboration, not co-optation (head teachers do not have a monopoly of wisdom, therefore vision building is a multi-way process with staff, students and parents and other stakeholders)
- make menus, not mandates (offer a choice of ways in which people can engage with teaching, learning and management successfully)
- use bureaucratic means to facilitate, not constrain, people's actions
- connect with the wider environment.

Leaders often need to prompt their colleagues to think critically about a current situation, i.e. to raise awareness of and questions about it, as is shown in Figure 10.1 (page 153), by reflecting with colleagues what are the current problems they and their students are encountering, what are the sources of these problems, how these might be addressed, and what are the particular values that the school wants to sustain, whatever changes it wants to make or is required to make.

Figure 10.1 Leading change through engaging people with learning

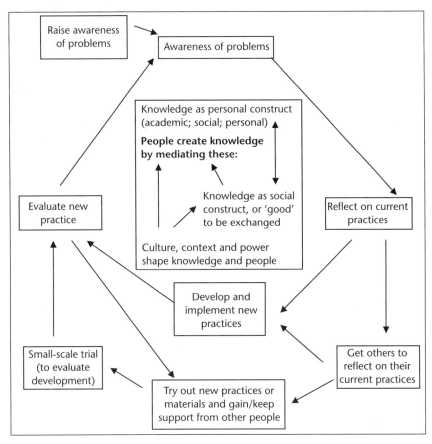

Actually bringing about change can be described through a political model as well as through a modernist or systems model. The former involves leaders in negotiating with staff, parents and students in a variety of transformational and transactional ways to engage them in developing teaching and learning and organizational processes to meet their needs, while at the same time proposing and modifying agenda of changes to policy or practice. To achieve this, leaders need to listen carefully to what other members of a school community are saying about the process of change and the goals they want to achieve and how these can be accommodated within the demands being made of the school by pressures in its external socio-political contexts. Of course autocratic leaders can simply impose changes but this is likely to lead to resistance by other members of a community – as is discussed elsewhere.

Negotiated approaches to change are not a narrowly instrumental process that can be portrayed as a series of steps or stages, but a complex process through which leaders of change gradually acquire greater access to power through gaining greater support for their proposals from their community, be it a school or a department or a class. As a consequence of this negotiation the original proposals are likely to be reshaped to take account of the interests of the different supporters of it. This is a normal rather than a pathological process, indicating a flexibility by the change leaders to acknowledge cultural pressures and the value of other people's insights rather than an indication of their moral turpitude in abandoning principled ideas. It often leads to them building temporary or longer-term alliances with a variety of people, especially those holding senior formal status, in order to gain access to sufficient power to implement the changes they want. Figure 10.2 tries to capture the major lines of a political model for implementing change.

Figure 10.2 Building alliances to implement change

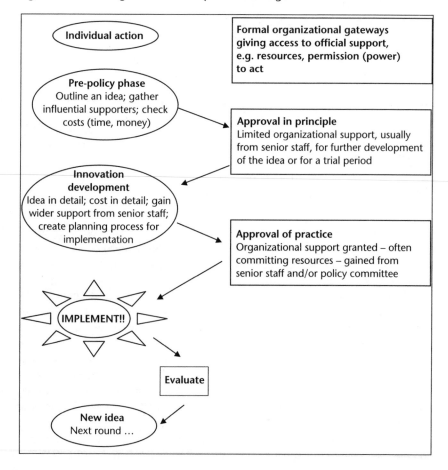

Leaders need to have sufficient expert technical knowledge to guide and help their colleagues to bring about change successfully (Busher and Barker 2003). In this case technical knowledge refers to knowledge about organizational processes as well as about learning and teaching and, where relevant, specific subject knowledge. Reeves *at al.* (2001) point out that an important element of this is knowledge of planning and development processes.

A modernist model of this change process is portrayed in Figure 10.3.

Figure 10.3 A modernist model for bringing about change and improvement

AUDIT: Where are you now? What is your current situation – professional knowledge, knowledge through experience, skills? What external factors create pressure on you?

GOALS: Where do you want to get to? Where do you expect to get to?

MONITORING EVALUATING PROGRESS: How will you know if you are making progress to your goals (benchmarking)? How will you know when you have arrived (targets)?

PROCESS: How will you get there? What is the time scale?
- critical path development planning/target setting
- working with colleagues; collegiality (culture)
- assessing the skills of colleagues (appraisal/mentoring) and professions development
- decision-making through consultation and negotiation
- managing the environment
- refining roles, rules, tasks and procedures
- budgeting and managing resources
- managing time effectively
- managing students – learning and teaching
- managing the curriculum

Fidler (1996: 99) locates this process as part of strategic planning in order to emphasize the interactivity between internal change processes in organizations and the external environments of those institutions. He views strategic planning as 'an attempt to impose patterns of order on incremental discontinuities by keeping long term objectives (where are we going?) in view when taking short term decisions (how do we get there?)'. Linking internal changes in a school or department to changes taking place in its external contexts gives criteria of purpose against which strategies of change can be evaluated and helps to avoid introducing changes unnecessarily or inappropriately. Alternatively strategic planning or future scenarios building can be perceived as merely modernist approaches to living with uncertainty and so at best offer a heuristic for exploring different routes that people in a community, school or department might take. None the less, the successful implementation of change, whether small or large scale, requires a certain degree of planning to establish when and how particular elements of a project will be constructed and implemented and how progress with the project will be assessed, as well as how the success of the project will be evaluated.

Change is costly in a number of different ways, not least in challenging current certainties held by staff, students and parents individually and collectively in a school, one of the reasons that some people resist change, as is discussed in Chapter 6. Leaders need to find ways of helping people to feel comfortable with intended changes and the processes of change in order to decrease the levels of opposition to the proposed developments. This could be described as a subtle or manipulative use of power to construct a supportive arena in which agenda for development can be discussed by departmental or school staff colleagues or students and through which various resources can be made available to support the processes of change as well as the actual intended change itself. One means of doing this is to engage colleagues in helping to evaluate what developments need to be undertaken, as is shown in Figure 10.4, and what priority each has. In many ways this process bears a lot of similarities to action research (Somekh 2000) or action learning approaches to managing change, especially when these are carried out by groups of people where leadership is genuinely collegial rather than hierarchic.

Figure 10.4 Using evaluation to drive change

What is the problem? • context
                    • scope
                    • time scale
                    • centrality to purpose

What do I need to know? What do I know already?

What alternative solutions might be possible?

Which solution is preferred? What are its benefits/intentions?
                    What are its costs? • money (material resources)
                                        • people
                                        • time
                                        • opportunity costs

How can the solution be:
• implemented
• monitored?

Evaluating the processes and outcomes.

What is the new problem now?

In IQEA projects evaluation in the form of a 'conditions survey' is a first step in bringing about change to find out whether members of that community find the working environment or culture in a school or department supportive of learning or discouraging (Beresford 2003). This not only helps to diagnose what problems need to be addressed but also where barriers to change might lie. This, in turn, potentially creates an arena into which staff, and students, too, can be drawn to discuss the implications of the evaluation for developing changes in policy and practice, thereby raising their critical awareness of the dilemmas involved in managing the school or department and also giving them an opportunity to share in constructing responses to those dilemmas. It forms part of a process that is discussed more fully elsewhere in this book but can be summed up as:

- developing authentic relationships (Hopkins *et al.* 1997a) includes gaining trust (Blase and Blase 1994; Hopkins 2001) among all participants in a school
- involvement of members of schools and departments, staff in particular but students and parents, too, in policy-making (Wallace *et al.* 1997)
- mentoring, appraisal and professional development (Moyles *et al.* 1998)
- critical self-reflection on practice by teams of teachers (Hopkins 2001)
- distributed leadership (Gronn 2000)
- engaging students actively in the evaluation and processes of change (Pickering 1997; Flutter and Rudduck 2004; Rudduck *et al.* 1996; Fielding 2004)

The construction of particular cultures in a department or school helps staff to collaborate in engaging with the problems they are confronting – even if within those discourses are held asymmetrical power relationships because promoted post-holders have more formal power (authority) than do other members of the group or community working on the problem or considering the possibilities of development.

However, there is another element to collaborative development by support staff and teachers that offers a fertile arena for curriculum development: the cross-school network. Busher and Hodgkinson (1996) point out the positive value that many teachers gave to being able to work together with colleagues, not only in their own schools but across schools to develop elements of the curriculum. The NCSL (National College for School Leadership) for England offers considerable opportunities for this networking for senior and middle leaders in schools. Unfortunately teachers are still reliant for developing such networks on attending courses, part-funded by another central government quango, the Teacher Development Agency

(TDA), at a university or other provider of in-service education, unless their schools happen to be part of an inter-school network, which may be web-based.

One local education authority in England provided inter-school networking for teacher development in various ways as part of a school improvement programme (Watling *et al.* 2003). LA inspectors linked to particular schools helped to run residential courses and workshop sessions for teachers in the programme and acted as critical friends and mentors to individual school improvement projects. The LA set up an inter-school learning network to keep schools and teachers in the programme in touch with each other. This eventually became web-based. As part of the programme the LA sponsored joint staff development sessions for participating schools. These were a notable success because of the high quality inputs from university staff and guest speakers and from experienced school leaders who showed practically how ideas for improving teaching and learning could be applied in classrooms. They also provided an arena in which teachers could share ideas with colleagues from other schools. When teachers criticized workshops, it was for not keeping a balance between new ideas, their practical application, and participant engagement in working out strategies for action.

From the foregoing discussion, then, the key parameters for developing inclusive learning and teaching in schools are probably the following:

- leadership and decision-making – by whom, with whom – and the distribution of power, authority and creativity
- values – for whom are schools being developed and for what purposes – and the impact of government policy and social contexts on schools
- creating a data-rich environment to monitor the success of practice
- organizational cultures – creating inclusive and engaging learning communities through modifying and developing school and classroom conditions
- staff development – sustaining work-related and personal and social growth
- building capacity for academic, personal, social and emotional learning and leading
- partnership with parents to sustain learning
- networking learning – schools and colleges working together to improve learning.

Establishing a culture of inclusion and social justice

This section explores what might be a research agenda for establishing the extent to which an institution can be perceived as providing a socially just environment for its members. It proposes an iterative approach for monitoring the culture of a school to record the extent to which it exhibits attributes of social justice, thereby revealing how power is distributed and used in whose interests in a school. Although this focus is on formal educational organizations, that is not to overlook the importance of carrying out similar monitoring of informal educational processes. Figure 10.5 identifies seven aspects of the processes of education organizations that need to be monitored to sustain the development of socially just education.

Figure 10.5 Seven aspects of schooling to monitor for establishing socially just education

1. How social and organisational systems and structures (Giddens 1984) shape how power (symbolic and physical resources) flows around the social frameworks into which it is locked.
2. Consider whether the policy and social contexts of schooling focus on transforming society or reproducing it and in the interests of whom or whose society/community/culture.
3. Analyse the value frameworks and repertoire of skills that leaders deploy as mediators of policy and social contexts to their staff and students: what is the quality of leaders' relationships with their colleagues, students and parents?
4. Voice and people's identities … what are members of the school community saying, where can these be heard, and how can their needs be met in terms that are meaningful to them?
5. Evaluating the organizational culture/sub-cultures of a school and how these are manifested in rules, ceremonies and language, and enacted by members of the school community: to what extent is social justice reflected in the actions and processes sanctioned by that culture?
6. To what extent/in what ways are participants in a school encouraged to engage in decision-making at many levels by asserting their voices, identities and agency?
7. Leadership … and therefore issues around power and how it is used and distributed in organizations (e.g. different types of leadership).

Social justice can be enacted in a variety of ways in a variety of situations related to education according to work by Cribb and Gewirtz (2003), Tett (2003), Riddell (2003) and Vincent (2003). These ways can be categorized as creating the following:

- distributive social justice – allocating goods/services on an equitable basis
- administrative social justice – bureaucracy – operating systems 'fairly'

- associative or affiliative social justice – right to form groups without hindrance
- representative social justice – right to voice views freely and to have them heard
- cultural social justice – acceptance of difference without discrimination.

Riddell (2003) argued that administrative or procedural justice has several different facets, some of which are in tension with others – see Table 10.1 – which she developed from the work of Mashaw (1983) and Kirp (1982). Work carried out in a school by staff and students could be considered in the light of these models of procedural justice to evaluate how well it met these criteria and what aspects of it needed further development.

Table 10.1 Six normative models of procedural justice

Type	Decision-making	Legitimating goal	Mode of accountability
Bureacracy	Applying rules	Accuracy	Hierarchy
Professionalism	Applying knowledge	Public service	Collegiality
Legality	Weighing arguments	Fairness	Independence
Managerialism	Focus on organisational needs	Effectiveness	Performance
Consumerism	Active choice	Consumer satisfaction	Codes of practice
Markets	Price mechanism	Profit/efficiency	Commercial viability

(source: Riddell 2003)

The following table (Table 10.2 on page 161) takes the categories of types of social justice and suggests how they might be applied to different aspects of schooling in order to help members of a school community consider the extent to which they are constructing socially just education.

Depending on how participants experience school processes from their own perspectives, actions that might seem quite reasonable to one group of people in a school could be perceived as unjust forms of control/discipline (Foucault 1977) to others. So, for example, procedures for countering truancy may be experienced as a means of control by students and parents – being forced to comply with bureaucratic procedures and legal rules from which they feel alienated – and not as a socially just way of supporting society's needs or those of other members of the school community, although the teachers managing these processes may perceive themselves as having acted fairly (justly according to the rules prescribed by the macro-society and institutional policy).

Table 10.2 Social justice and education: welcoming the marginalized

Types of justice	Relationships with			Pedagogy	Pastoral care	Curriculum	'Budget'/ resource allocation	Administration ** student grouping
	students	staff	parents					
Distributive* justice								
Cultural* justice								
Associative* justice								
Representative social justice								
Administrative** justice								

Notes: * These aspects are derived from Gewirtz (2002)
       ** This aspect is derived from Riddell (2002)

Peroration

At the core of understanding how people work together in school communities and sub-communities are their interactions individually and in groups to implement values that they consider important with whatever resources they can lay their hands on. How they gain access to resources or prevent other people gaining access is a matter of the politics in which people engage in support of their interests and those of others and agenda in the framework of the cultures of the communities of which they have membership. These cultures represent the core values that those communities have constructed for themselves to define and identify their members as separate from other communities or sub-communities. Discussions of change and social justice seem to bring these issues to the fore as they highlight the asymmetrical power relationships that are embedded in organizations and raise questions about in whose interests is power used in those organizations. Such concerns are not only of key importance to leaders of schools and departments but also to those who, in some way or for some reason, are marginalized in the social and curriculum processes of schooling. Leaders of schools at whatever level, from classrooms to governors' meetings, who fail to address adequately such issues leave schools continuing to reproduce the existing injustices and inequalities of society, if not making them worse, leaving new generations of some students to feel as equally disaffected as their parents, and new generations of teachers coping with the same confrontations and socially unacceptable behaviours from some students as have their predecessors.

References

Allix, N.M. (2000) Transformational leadership: Democratic or despotic? *Educational Management and Administration*, 28(1): 7–20.

Alvesson, M. (1993) *Cultural Perspectives on Organisations*, Cambridge: Cambridge University Press.

Aubrey, C., David, T., Godfrey, R. and Thompson, L. (2000) *Early Childhood Educational Research: Issues in Methodology and Ethics*, London: RoutledgeFalmer.

Bacharach, S. (1983) Notes on a political theory of educational organizations, in A. Westoby (ed.) (1988) *Culture and Power in Organisations*, Milton Keynes: Open University Press.

Bacharach, S. and Lawler, E. (1980) *Power and Politics in Organisations*, San Francisco: Jossey-Bass.

Ball, S.J. (1987) *The Micro-politics of the School*, London: Methuen.

Ball, S.J. (1989) Micro-politics versus management: Towards a sociology of school organization, in S. Walker and L. Barton (eds) *Politics and the Processes of Schooling*, Milton Keynes: Open University Press.

Ball, S.J and Bowe, R. (1992) Subject departments and the implementation of National Curriculum policy: An overview of the issues, *Journal of Curriculum Studies*, 24(2): 97–115.

Beare, H., Caldwell, B. and Milikan, R. (1989) *Creating an Excellent School: Some New Management Techniques*, London: Routledge.

Begley, P.T. (1999a) Introduction, in P.T. Begley and P.E. Leonard (eds) (1999) *The Values of Educational Administration*, London: Falmer Press.

Begley, P.T. (1999b) Academic and practitioner perspectives on values, in P.T. Begley and P.E. Leonard (eds) (1999) *The Values of Educational Administration*, London: Falmer Press.

Benjamin, S. (2002) *The Micro-politics of Inclusive Education*, Buckingham: Open University Press.

Bennett, N. (2001) Power, structure and culture: An organizational view of school effectiveness and school improvement, in N. Bennett and A. Harris (eds) (2001) *School Effectiveness and School Improvement: Searching for the Elusive Partnership*, London: Continuum.

Bennett, N., Wise, C., Woods, P.A. and Newton, W. (2003) Leading from the middle: A review and analysis of the evidence. Paper given at the British Educational Research Association Annual Conference, Edinburgh, 14–16 September.

Beresford, J. (2003) Developing students as effective learners: The student conditions for school improvement, *School Effectiveness and School Improvement*, June 2003.

Bhabha, H. (1994) *The Location of Culture*, London: Routledge.

Blase, J. and Anderson, G.L. (1995) *The Micro-politics of Educational Leadership: From Control to Empowerment*, London: Cassell.

Blase, J. and Blase, J. (1994) *Empowering Teachers: What Successful Principals Do*, Thousand Oaks, CA: Corwin.

Blau, P. (1964) *Exchange and Power in Social Life*, New York: John Wiley.

Bottery, M. (2003) The leadership of learning communities in a culture of unhappiness, paper given to the ESRC Seminar Series 'Challenging the orthodoxy of school leadership: Towards a new theoretical perspective', National College for School Leadership, UK, June 2003.

Bourdieu, P. (1990) *The Logic of Practice*, tr. Richard Nice, Cambridge: Polity Press.

Bourdieu, P. and Passeron, J.C. (1977) *Reproduction in Education: Society and Culture*, London: Sage.

Bourdieu, P., Passeron, J.C. and de Saint Martin, M. (1994) *Academic Discourses*, Polity Press: Cambridge.

Bowe, R. and Ball, S. with Gold, A. (1992) *Reforming Education and Changing Schools: Case Studies in Policy Sociology*, London: Routledge.

Bradley, C. and Roaf, C. (1995) Meeting special educational needs in the secondary school: a team approach, *Support for Learning*, 10(2): 93–9.

Brown, M. (1996) Leadership for school improvement: The changing role of the head of department. Paper given at the BEMAS Research Conference, Robinson College, Cambridge.

Burns, J.M. (1978) *Leadership*, London: Harper Row.

Burns, T. (1955) The reference of conduct in small groups: Cliques and cabals in occupational milieux, *Human Relations*, 8: 467–86.

Busher, H. (1989) Making sense of reality: A case study of one teacher reflecting on her practice, in P. Lomax (ed.) (1989) *The Management of Change*, BERA Dialogues 1, Clevedon: Multilingual Matters.

Busher, H. (1992) The politics of working in secondary schools: Some teachers' perspectives on their schools as organizations. Unpublished PhD thesis, Leeds: University of Leeds, School of Education.

Busher, H. (1998) Educational leadership and management: Contexts, theory and practice, in P. Clough (ed.) (1998) *Managing Special and Inclusive Education*, London: Paul Chapman.

Busher, H. (2001) The micro-politics of change, improvement and effectiveness in schools, in N. Bennett and A. Harris (eds) *School Effectiveness and School Improvement: Searching for the Elusive Partnership*, London: Continuum.

Busher, H. (2002) Being and becoming a subject leader: Histories and ethnographies. Paper given at the British Educational Research Association (BERA) Annual Conference, Exeter, September 2002.

Busher, H. (2005a) Being a middle leader: exploring professional identities, *School Leadership and Management*, 25(1): 137–54.

Busher, H. (2005b) The project of the other: Developing inclusive learning communities in schools, *Oxford Review of Education*, 31(3): 459–77.

Busher, H. and Barker, B. (2003) The crux of leadership: Shaping school culture by contesting the policy contexts and practices of teaching and learning, *Educational Management and Administration*, 31(1): 51–65.

Busher, H. and Blease, D. (2000) Growing collegial cultures in subject departments in secondary schools: working with science staff, *School Leadership and Management*, 20(1): 99–112.

Busher, H. and Harris, A. with Wise, C. (2000) *Subject Leadership for School Improvement*, London: Paul Chapman.

Busher, H. and Hodgkinson, K. (1996) Co-operation and tension between autonomous schools: a study of interschool networking, *Educational Review*, 48(1): 55–64.

Busher, H. and Saran, R. (1992) *Teachers' Conditions of Employment: A Study in the Politics of School Management*, Bedford Way Series, London: Kogan Page.

Busher, H. and Saran, R. (1995) Managing with support staff, in H. Busher and R. Saran (eds) *Managing Teachers as Professionals in Schools*, London: Kogan Page.

Busher, H. and Saran, R. (2000) Managing with support staff, in K. Stott and V. Trafford (eds) (2000) *Partnerships: Shaping the Future of Education*, London: Middlesex University Press.

Carney, F. (2004) More parental rapport, *Times Educational Supplement*, 30 April 2004: 6.

Clark, D. (1996) *Schools as Learning Communities: Transforming Education*, London: Cassell.

Coles, M. and Chilvers, P. (2005) *Education and Islam: Developing a Culturally Inclusive Curriculum*, Leicester: Leicester City Council, School Development Support Agency.

Cooper, P., Drummond, M., Hart, S., Lovey, J. and McLaughlin, C. (2000) *Positive Alternatives to Exclusion*, London: RoutledgeFalmer.

Cooper, P. and McIntyre, D. (1996) *Effective Teaching and Learning: Teachers' and Students' Perspectives*, Milton Keynes: Open University Press.

Creemers, B. (1994) *The Effective Classroom*, London: Cassell.

Cribb, A. and Gewirtz, S. (2003) Towards a sociology of just practices: An analysis of plural conceptions of justice, in C. Vincent (ed.) (2003) *Social Justice, Education and Identity*, London: RoutledgeFalmer.

Crozier, G. (2000) Excluded parents: The deracialization of parental involvement. Paper given at the British Education Research Association Annual Conference, Cardiff, September 2000.

Day, C., Harris, A., Hadfield, M., Tolley, H. and Beresford, J. (2000) *Leading Schools in Times of Change*, Buckingham: Open University Press.

Day, C., Whitaker, P. and Johnson, D. (1990) *Managing Primary Schools in the 1990s: A Professional Development Approach*, 2nd edn, London: Paul Chapman.

Deal, T.E. (1988) *Corporate Cultures: The Rites and Rituals of Corporate Life*, Harmondsworth: Penguin.

Demie, F. (2004) Achievement of Black Caribbean pupils: Good practice in Lambeth schools, *British Educational Research Journal*, 31(4): 481–508.

DfEE (1998) *Draft Guidance on Home School Agreements*, London: DfEE.

DfES (2004) *Every Child Matters: Change for Children*, London: DfES.

Dimmock, C. and Walker, A. (1998) Towards comparative educational administration: Building the case for cross-cultural school based approach, *Journal of Educational Administration*, 36(4): 379–96.

Donnelly, C. (2004) Constructing the ethos of tolerance and respect in an integrated school: The role of teachers, *British Educational Research Journal*, 30(2): 263–78.

Driessen, G., Smit, F. and Sleegers, P. (2004) Parental involvement and educational achievement, *British Educational Research Journal*, 31(4): 509–32.

Duignan, P. and McPherson, R. (1992) *Educative Leadership: Practical Theory for New Administrators and Managers*, London: Falmer Press.

Edwards, A.D., Fitz, J. and Whitty, G. (1989) *The State and Private Education: An Evaluation of the Assisted Places Scheme*, London: Falmer Press.

Etzioni, A. (1961) *A Comparative Analysis of Complex Organisations*, New York: Free Press.

Fidler, B. (1996) *Strategic Planning for School Improvement*, London: Pitman.

Fielding, M. (2001) Target setting, policy pathology and student perspectives: Learning to labour in new times, in M. Fielding (ed.) (2001) *Taking Education Really Seriously: Four Years Hard Labour*, London: RoutledgeFalmer.

Fielding, M. (2004) Transformative approaches to student voice: Theoretical underpinnings, recalcitrant realities, *British Educational Research Journal*, 30(2): 295–310.

Flutter, J. and Rudduck, J. (2004) *Consulting Pupils: What's In It for Schools*, London: RoutledgeFalmer.

Foucault, M. (1975) *Birth of the Clinic: An Archaeology of Medical Perception*, tr. A.M. Sheridan, New York: Vintage/Random House.

Foucault, M. (1976) Truth and Power, in C. Gordon (ed.) (1980) *Power/Knowledge: Selected Interviews and Other Writings by Michel Foucault, 1972–1977*, New York: Pantheon.

Foucault, M. (1977) *Discipline and Punish: The Birth of the Prison*, tr. A. Sheridan, London: Allen Lane.

Foucault, M. (1986) Disciplinary power and subjection, in S. Lukes (ed.) (1986) *Power*, Oxford: Blackwell.

Francis, B. and Archer, L. (2005) British–Chinese pupils' and parents' constructions of the value of education, *British Educational Research Journal*, 31(1): 89–108.

French, J. and Raven, B. (1968) The bases of social power, in D. Cartwright and A. Zander (eds) *Group Dynamics, Research and Theory*, London: Tavistock Press.

Frost, D. and Durrant, J. (2003) Teacher leadership: Rationale, strategy and impact, *School Leadership and Management*, 23(2): 173–86.

Fullan, M. (2001) *The New Meaning of Educational Change*, 3rd edn, London: RoutledgeFalmer.

Fullan, M. (2003) *The Moral Imperative of School Leadership*, Thousand Oaks, CA: Corwin Press.

Fullan, M. and Hargreaves, A. (1992) *What's Worth Fighting For in Your School? Working Together for Improvement*, Buckingham: Open University Press.

Galton, M., Gray, J. and Rudduck, J. (1999) *The Impact of School Transitions on Pupil Progress and Attainment, Research Report No. 131*, London: DfEE.

Gamble, A. (1996) *Hayek: The Iron Cage of Liberty*, Cambridge: Polity Press.

Gersten, F. (1995) The pupil experience: A view from both sides, in D. Thomas (ed.) (1995) *Teachers' Stories*, Buckingham: Open University Press.

Gewirtz, S. (2002) Paper given in an ESRC seminar on education and social justice, Institute of Education, London.

Ghosn, I. (1998) Connecting to classroom realities: Curriculum, methods and the hidden curriculum as agents of peace, in I. Ghosn and E. Samia (eds) (1998) *Weaving the Fabric of Peace: Tolerance, Justice and the Child*, Byblos: Lebanese American University, Centre for Peace and Justice Education.

Gibb, C. (1947) The principles and traits of leadership, in C. Gibb (ed.) (1969) *Leadership*, Harmondsworth: Penguin.

Giddens, A. (1979) *Central Problems in Social Theory: Action, Structure and Contradiction in Social Analysis*, Berkeley: University of California Press.

Giddens, A. (1984) *The Constitution of Society*, Cambridge: Polity Press.

Giddens, A. (1991) *Modernity and Self-identity: Self and Society in the Late Modern Age*, Cambridge: Polity Press.

Glatter, R. (1997) Context and capability in educational management, *Educational Management and Administration*, 25(2): 191–202.

Glover, D., Gleeson, D., Gough, G. and Johnson, M. (1998) The meaning of management: The development needs of middle managers in secondary schools, *Educational Management and Administration*, 26(3): 181–95.

Goleman, D. (1995) *Emotional Intelligence*, New York: Bantam.

Goodson, I. (1992) *Studying Teachers' Lives*, London: Routledge.

Grace, G. (1995) *School Leadership: Beyond Educational Management – An Essay in Policy Scholarship*, London: Falmer Press.

Grace, G., Bell, D. and Browne, B. (1996) St Michael's Roman Catholic Comprehensive School, in National Commission on Education (1996) *Success Against the Odds: Effective Schools in Disadvantaged Areas*, London: Routledge.

Gray, L. (1991) *Marketing Education*, Buckingham: Open University Press.

Greenfield, T. (1993) Against group mind: an anarchistic theory of organization, in T. Greenfield and P. Ribbins (eds) *Greenfield on Educational Administration*, London: Routledge.

Gronn, P. (2000) Distributed properties: A new architecture for leadership, *Educational Management and Administration*, 28(3): 317–38.

Gronn, P. (2002) Distributed leadership as a unit of analysis, *The Leadership Quarterly*, 13: 423–51.

Gronn, P. (2003) Leadership: Who needs it? Paper given to the ESRC Seminar Series 'Challenging the orthodoxy of school leadership: Towards a new theoretical perspective', University of Birmingham, UK, February 2003.

Guardian (2000) Mr Fixit's new mission, *Guardian*, 7 January.

Gunter, H., McGregor, D. and Gunter, B. (2001) Teachers as leaders: A case study, *Management in Education*, 15(1): 26–8.

Gunter, H. and Ribbins, P. (2002) Leadership studies in education: Towards a map of the field, *Educational Management Administration and Leadership*, 30(4): 387–416.

Habermas, J. (1996) *The Habermas Reader*, ed. William Outhwaite, Cambridge: Polity Press.

Hall, V. (1997) Managing staff, in B. Fidler, S. Russell and T. Simkins (eds) *Choices for Self-managing Schools*, London: Paul Chapman.

Hallinger, P. and Heck, R. (1999) Can leadership enhance school effectiveness? In T. Bush, L. Bell, R. Bolam, R. Glatter and P. Ribbins (eds) *Educational Management: Redefining Theory, Policy and Practice*, London: Paul Chapman.

Halpin, D. (2003) *Hope and Education: The Role of the Utopian Imagination*, London: RoutledgeFalmer.

Hannerz, U. (1992) *Cultural Complexity: Studies in the Social Organisation of Meaning*, New York: Columbia University Press.

Hardy, C. (1985) The nature of unobtrusive power, *Journal of Management Studies*, 22(4): 384–99.

Hargreaves, A. (1994) *Changing Teachers, Changing Times: Teachers' Work and Culture in the Post-modern Age,* London: Cassell.

Harris, A. (1999) *Effective Subject Leadership: A Handbook of Staff Development Activities,* London: David Fulton Press.

Harris, A. (2000) What works in school improvement? Lessons from the field and future directions, *Educational Research,* 42(1): 1–11.

Harrison, B.T. (1994) Applying critical ethics to educational management, *Educational Management and Administration,* 22(3): 175–83.

Hase, S., Davies, A. and Dick, B. (1999) *The Johari Window and the Dark Side of Organisations,* original ultiBase publication, http://ultibase.rmit. edu.au/Articles/aug99/hase1.htm (accessed 18 June 2004)

Hodgkinson, C. (1991) *Educational Leadership: The Moral Art,* Albany: State University of New York Press.

Hodgkinson, C. (1999) The triumph of the will: An exploration of certain fundamental problematics in administrative philosophy, in P.T. Begley and P.E. Leonard (eds) *The Values of Educational Administration,* London: Falmer Press.

Hodson, D. and Hodson, J. (1998) Science education as enculturation: Some implications for practice, *School Science Review,* 80(290): 17–24.

Hofstede, G. (1991) *Cultures and Organizations: Software of the Mind,* London: McGraw-Hill.

Holliday, A. (1994) *Appropriate Methodology and Social Context,* Cambridge: Cambridge University Press.

Holliday, A. (2004) *Intercultural Communication: An Advanced Resource Book,* London: Routledge.

Holliday, A. (2005) Small cultures – small identities: The richness of self in a changing world. Paper given at the conference on 'Interrogating Third Spaces in Language Teaching, Learning and Use', Leicester: Centre for English Language Teacher Education and Applied Linguistics, School of Education, University of Leicester.

Hollis, M. (1985) Of masks and men, in M. Carrithers, S. Collins and S. Lukes (eds) *The Category of the Person: Anthropology, Philosophy, History,* Cambridge: Cambridge University Press.

Homans, G. (1958) Social behaviour as exchange, *American Journal of Sociology,* 63(6): 597–606.

Hopkins, D. (2001) *Improving the Quality of Education for All,* London: David Fulton.

Hopkins, D., Ainscow, M. and West, M. (1994) *School Improvement in an Era of Change,* London: Cassell.

Hopkins, D., Ainscow, M. and West, M. (1997a) Improving the Quality of Education for All: Reflections on a school improvement project, *Topic,* Spring, 17.

Hopkins, D., West, M., Harris, A., Ainscow, M. and Beresford, J. (1997b) *Creating the Conditions for Classroom Improvement,* London: David Fulton.

Hopkins, D. and Reynolds, D. (2001) The past, present and future of school improvement: Towards the Third Age, *British Educational Research Journal*, 27(4): 459–75.

Howard, S. and Gill, J. (2000) The pebble in the pond: Children's constructions of power, politics and democratic citizenship, *Cambridge Journal of Education*, 30(3): 355–78.

Hoyle, E. (1981) Management and the school, Block 3, *E323 Management Processes in Schools*, Milton Keynes: Open University Press.

Hoyle, E. (1982) Micro-politics of educational organizations, *Educational Management and Administration*, 10(2): 87–98.

Hoyle, E. (1986) *The Politics of School Management*, London: Hodder and Stoughton.

Hoyle, E. and John, P.D. (1995) *Professional Knowledge and Professional Practice*, London: Cassell.

Hughes, M. (1985) Leadership in professionally staffed organizations, in M. Hughes, P. Ribbins and H. Thomas (eds) *Managing Education: The System and the Institution*, London: Holt Rinehart & Winston.

Ireson, J. and Hallam, S. (2001) *Ability Grouping in Education*, London: Paul Chapman/Sage.

James, C., Connolly, M., Dunning, G., and Elliott, T. (2006) *How very effective Primary Schools Work*, London: Paul Chapman.

Joyce, B., Calhoun, E. and Hopkins, D. (1997) *Models of Teaching: Tools for Learning*, London: Open University Press.

Kamel, O.M. (1998) Goals and problems of higher education, *Saudi Gazette*, 11 October.

Katzenmeyer, M. and Moller, G. (2001) *Awakening the Sleeping Giant: Helping Teachers Develop as Leaders*, 2nd edn, Thousand Oaks, CA: Corwin Press.

Kazmi, A. (1998) Ethics and professional values in business and industry in India, *Paradigm*, 1(2): 86–93.

Kazmi, A. and Hallan, V. (2005) Minority Ethnic Achievement Project and the Key Stage 3 National Strategy. Paper given at the seminar on 'School improvement and social justice', School of Education, University of Leicester, 26 January.

Kirp, D. (1982) Professionalism as a policy choice: British special education in comparative perspective, *World Politics*, 34(2): 137–74.

Krechevsky, M. and Stork, J. (2000) Challenging educational assumptions, *Cambridge Journal of Education*, 30(1): 57–74.

Lafleur, C. (1999) The meaning of time in P.T. Begley and P.E. Leonard (eds) (1999) *The Values of Educational Administration*, London: Falmer Press.

LaFontaine, J.S. (1985) Person and individual: Some anthropological reflections, in M. Carrithers, S. Collins and S. Lukes (eds) *The Category of the Person: Anthropology, Philosophy, History*, Cambridge: Cambridge University Press.

Lauder, H. and Hughes, D. (1999) *Trading in Futures: Why Markets in Education Don't Work*, Buckingham: Open University Press.

Lenski, G. (1986) Power and privilege, in S. Lukes (ed.) *Power*, Oxford: Blackwell.

Levinson, B.A., Foley, D.E. and Holland, D.C. (1996) *The Cultural Production of the Educated Person: Critical Ethnographies of Schooling and Local Practice*, Albany: State University of New York Press.

Linstead, S. (1993) Deconstruction of the study of organizations, in J. Hassard and M. Parker (eds) *Postmodernism and Organisations*, London: Sage.

Little, J.W. (1993) Teachers' professional development in a climate of educational reform, *Educational Evaluation and Policy Analysis*, 15(2): 129–51.

Lomax, P. (1990) An action research approach to developing staff in schools, in P. Lomax (ed.) (1990) *Managing Staff Development in Schools: An Action Research Approach*, BERA Dialogues 3, Clevedon: Multilingual Matters.

Louis, K., Marks, H. and Kruse, S. (1996) Teachers' professional community in restructuring schools, *American Educational Research Journal*, 33.

Loveless, T. (1999) *The Tracking Wars: State Reform Meets School Policy*, Washington: The Brookings Institution.

Lukes, S. (1974) *Power: A Radical View*, London: Macmillan Press.

Lukes, S. (1986) Introduction, in S. Lukes (ed.) *Power*, Oxford: Blackwell.

MacBeath, J. and MacDonald, A. (2000) Four dilemmas, three heresies and a matrix, in K.A. Riley and K.S. Louis (eds) *Leadership for Change and School Reform*, London: RoutledgeFalmer.

MacGilchrist, B., Myers, K. and Reed, J. (2004) *The Intelligent School*, 2nd edn, London: Sage.

McGill, I. and Beaty, L. (2001) *Action Learning: A Guide for Professional, Management and Educational Development*, rev. 2nd edn, London: Kogan Page.

McGregor, J. (2000) The challenge of collaboration: What encourages joint work between teachers? Paper presented at the BEMAS Research Conference, Robinson College, Cambridge, UK, July.

McMahon, A. (2001) A cultural perspective on school effectiveness, school improvement and teacher professional development, in A. Harris and N. Bennett (eds) *School Effectiveness and School Improvement: Alternative Perspectives*, London: Continuum.

Marsh, M. (1997) In conversation with Janet Ouston, in P. Ribbins (ed.) *Leaders and Leadership in the School, College and University*, London: Cassell.

Martin, P,. Creese, A., Bhatt, A. and Bhojani, N. (2004) *Complementary Schools and their Communities in Leicester*, Leicester: School of Education, University of Leicester.

Mashaw, J.L. (1983) *Bureaucratic Justice: Managing Social Security Disability Claims*, New Haven and London: Yale University Press.

Measor, L. and Sikes, P. (1992) Visiting lives: Ethics and methodology in life history, in I. Goodson (ed.) (1992) *Studying Teachers' Lives*, London: Routledge.

Moos, L. (2000) Global and national perspectives on leadership, in K.A. Riley and K.S. Louis (eds) *Leadership for Change and School Reform*, London: RoutledgeFalmer.

Morgan, G. (1986) *Images of Organisations*, New York: Sage.

Mortimore, P. (1993) School effectiveness and the management of effective learning and teaching, *School Effectiveness and School Improvement*, 4(4): 290–310.

Mortimore, P. and Whitty, G. (1997) *Can School Improvement Overcome the Effects of Disadvantage?* London: Institute of Education, University of London.

Moyles, J., Suschitsky, W. and Chapman, L. (1998) *Teaching Fledglings to Fly: Report on Mentoring in Primary Schools*, London: Association of Teachers and Lecturers.

Muijs, D. and Harris, A. (2003) Teacher leadership – improvement through empowerment? An overview of the literature, *Educational Management and Administration*, 31(4): 437–48.

Mullins, L.J., (1996) *Management and Organisational Behaviour*, London: Pitman Publishing.

Murphy, J. (1992) *The Landscape of Leadership Preparation*, Newbury Park, CA: Corwin Press.

Nesbitt, J. (2004) No cold feet for parents here, *Times Educational Supplement*, 26 November 2004: 7.

Nias, J. (1999) Becoming a primary school teacher, in J. Prosser (ed.) *School Culture*, London: Paul Chapman.

O'Connor, C. (1997) Dispositions towards (collective) struggle and educational resilience in the inner city: A case analysis of six African–American high school students, *American Educational Research Journal*, 34(4): 593–629.

Osler, A. and Vincent, K. (2003) *Girls and Exclusion: Rethinking the Agenda*, London: RoutledgeFalmer.

Osler, A., Watling, R. and Busher, H. (2000) *Reasons for Exclusion from School*, Research Report RR244, London: Department for Education and Employment.

Ouston, J. and Hood, S. (2000) *Home-School Agreements: A True Partnership?*, London: The Research and Information on Education Trust.

Parsons, T. (1986) Power and the social system, in S. Lukes (ed.) *Power*, Oxford: Blackwell.

Pickering, J. (1997) *Involving Pupils*, Research Matters, London: Institute of Education, University of London.

Plant, R. (1987) *Managing Change and Making it Stick*, London: Fontana.

Poster, C. (1976) *School Decision-making*, London: Heinemann.

Prosser, J. (1999) Introduction, in J. Prosser (ed.) *School Culture*, London: Paul Chapman.

Raham, H. (2003) Schools that make a difference: Twelve Canadian secondary schools in low-income settings. Paper given to the American Education Research Association, San Diego, April 2004.

Randell, G., Packard, P. and Slater, J. (1990) *Staff Appraisal: A First Step to Effective Leadership*, 3rd edn, London: Institute of Personnel Management.

Ranson, J. (2000) Recognizing the pedagogy of voice in a learning community, *Educational Management and Administration*, 28(3): 263–80.

Reay, D. (1998) Micro-politics in the 1990s: Staff relationships in secondary schooling, *Journal of Education Policy*, 13(2): 179–96.

Reeves, J., McCall, J. and MacGilchrist, B. (2001) Change leadership: Planning, conceptualization and perception, in J. MacBeath and P. Mortimore (eds) *Improving School Effectiveness*, Buckingham: Open University Press.

Reynolds, D. (1998) The study and remediation of ineffective schools, in L. Stoll and K. Myers (eds) *No Quick Fixes: Perspectives on Schools in Difficulty*, London: Falmer Press.

Ribbins, P. (1985) Organization theory and the study of educational institutions, in M. Hughes, P. Ribbins and H. Thomas (eds) *Managing Education: The System and the Institution*, London: Holt Rinehart & Winston.

Ribbins, P. (1992) What professionalism means to teachers. Paper given at the British Educational Management and Administration Society (BEMAS) Fourth Research Conference, University of Nottingham, July 1992.

Ribbins, P. (1997) *Leaders and Leadership in the School, College and University*, London: Cassell.

Ribbins, P. (1999) Foreword, in P.T. Begley and P.E. Leonard (eds) *The Values of Educational Administration*, London: Falmer Press.

Riddell, S. (2002) Paper given in an ESRC seminar on education and social justice, Institute of Education, London.

Riddell, S. (2003) Special educational needs and procedural justice in England and Scotland, in C. Vincent (ed.) *Social Justice, Education and Identity*, London: RoutledgeFalmer.

Riley, K. (2004) Leading challenging urban schools: Demands, dilemmas and dreams. Paper given to the America Educational Research Association, April 2004.

Riley, K.A., Docking, J. and Rowles, D. (2000) Caught between local education authorities: Making a difference through their leadership, in

K.A. Riley and K.S. Louis (eds) *Leadership for Change and School Reform*, London: RoutledgeFalmer.

Riley, K. and Rustique-Forrester, E. (2002) *Working with Disaffected Students*, London: Paul Chapman.

Robbins, S.P. (2003) *Organizational Behaviour*, 10th edn, Englewood Cliffs, NJ: Prentice Hall.

Rudduck, J. and Flutter, J. (2000) Pupils' participation and pupils' perspective: Carving a new order of experience, *Cambridge Journal of Education*, 30(1): 75–89.

Rudduck, J., Wallace, G. and Chaplain, R. (1996) *School Improvement: What Can Pupils Tell Us?* London: David Fulton.

Ryan, J. (2003) Greenfield and the post-modern: Order, anarchy and inquiry in educational administration, in R.M.B. Macmillan (ed.) *Questioning Leadership: The Greenfield Legacy*, London, Ontario: The Althouse Press.

Sammons, P. and Mortimore, P. (1997) *Effective Departments: Effective Schools*, London: Routledge.

Schein, E. (1990) Organizational culture, *American Psychologist*, 45(2): 109–19.

Schein, E. (1992) *Organisational Culture and Leadership*, 2nd edn, San Francisco, CA: Jossey-Bass.

Schon, D. (1987) *Educating the Reflective Practitioner: Towards a New Design for Teaching and Learning in the Professions*, San Francisco, CA: Jossey-Bass.

Senge, P. (1990) *The Fifth Discipline*, New York: Doubleday.

Sergiovanni, T.J. (1992) *Moral Leadership: Getting to the Heart of School Improvement*, San Francisco, CA: Jossey-Bass.

Sergiovanni, T.J. (1994) *Building Community in Schools*, San Francisco, CA: Jossey-Bass.

Sergiovanni, T.J. (1995) *The Principalship: A Reflective Perspective*, Boston, MA: Allyn & Bacon.

Sergiovanni, T.J. (2001) *Leadership: What's in it for Schools?* London: RoutledgeFalmer.

Shaw, M. (2003) 'Seva' is secret of Sikh success, *Times Educational Supplement*, 28 March 2003: 12.

Simkins, T. (1997) Managing resources, in H. Tomlinson (ed.) *Managing Continual Professional Development in Schools*, London: Paul Chapman.

Siskin, L. (1991) Departments as different worlds: subject subcultures in secondary schools, *Education Administration Quarterly*, 27(2): 134–60.

Siskin, L. (1994) *Realms of Knowledge: Academic Departments in Secondary Schools*, London: Falmer Press.

Slee, R. (1991) Learning initiatives to include all students in regular schools, in M. Ainscow (ed.) *Effective Schools for All*, London: David Fulton.

Smith, M.E. (2003) Changing an organization's culture: Correlates of success and failure, *Leadership and Organization Development Journal*, 24(5/6): 249–64.

Smylie, M. (1994) Redesigning teachers' work: Connections to the classroom, in L. Darling-Hammond (ed.) *Review of Research in Education*, Washington, DC: American Educational Research Association.

Smyth, J., Dow, A., Hattam, R., Reid, A. and Shacklock, G. (2000) *Teachers' Work in a Globalising Economy*, London: Falmer Press.

Somekh, B. (2000) Changing conceptions of action research, in H. Altrichter and J. Elliott (eds) *Images of Educational Change*, Buckingham: Open University Press.

Starratt, R.J. (1999) Moral dimensions of leadership, in P.T. Begley and P.E. Leonard (eds) *The Values of Educational Administration*, London: Falmer Press.

Stoll, L. and Fink, D. (1998) The cruising school: The unidentified ineffective school, in L. Stoll and K. Myers (eds) *No Quick Fixes: Perspectives on Schools in Difficulty*, London: Falmer Press.

Stout, R.T., Tallerico, M. and Scribner, K.P. (1994) Values: The 'what?' of the politics of education, in J.D. Scribner (ed.) *Politics of Education Association Yearbook 1994*, London: Taylor & Francis.

Tannenbaum, R. and Schmidt, W. (1973) How to choose a leadership pattern, *Harvard Business Review*, 51(3): 162–80.

Teacher Training Agency (1998) *National Qualifications for Subject Leaders*, London: HMSO.

Tett, L. (2003) Education and community health: Identity, social justice and lifestyle issues in communities, in C. Vincent (ed.) *Social Justice, Education and Identity*, London: RoutledgeFalmer.

Thomas, D. (1995) Teachers' stories studies, in D. Thomas (ed.) *Teachers' Stories*, Buckingham: Open University Press.

Thrupp, M. (1998) Exploring the politics of blame: School inspection and its contestation in New Zealand and England, *Comparative Education*, 34(2): 195–208.

Thrupp, M. (1999) *Schools Making a Difference: Let's Be Realistic!* Buckingham: Open University Press.

Times Educational Supplement (2004) Homeless and helpless, *TES*, 4 June 2004: 4.

Torres, C.A. (1999) Critical theory and political sociology of education: Arguments, in T.S. Popkewitz and L. Fendler (eds) *Critical Theories in Education*, London: Routledge.

Trompenaars, F. and Woolliams, P. (2003) A new framework for managing change across cultures, *Journal of Change Management*, 3(4): 361–74.

van der Westhuizen, P. (1996) Resistance to change in educational organizations. Paper given at the Fifth Quadrennial Research Conference of the British Educational Management and Administration Society, Cambridge University, Cambridge, UK, July 1996.

Vincent, C. (2000) *Including Parents? Education, Citizenship and Parental Agency*, Buckingham: Open University Press.

Vincent, C. (2003) Introduction, in C. Vincent (ed.) *Social Justice, Education and Identity*, London: RoutledgeFalmer.

Wallace, R., Engel, D. and Mooney, J. (1997) *The Learning School: A Guide to Vision-based Leadership*, Thousand Oaks, CA: Corwin Press.

Watling, R., Busher, H., Brundrett, M., Harrison, J. and Wortley, A. with Stevenson, H. (2003) *External Evaluation of the Nottinghamshire County Council IQEA Project*, Leicester: University of Leicester, School of Education.

Watson, L. (1969) Office and expertise in the secondary school, *Educational Research*, 11(2): 104–12.

Weber, M. (1947) *The Theory of Social and Economic Organisations* (tr. A.M. Henderson and H. Talcott Parsons), Glencoe, Il: Free Press.

Weber, S. and Mitchell, C. (1999) Teacher identity in popular culture, in J. Prosser (ed.) *School Culture*, London: Paul Chapman.

Wells, S.A. (1996) African-American students' view of school choice, in B. Fuller and R. Elmore with G. Orfield (eds) *Who Chooses? Who Loses? Culture, Institutions and the Unequal Effects of School Choice*, New York: Teachers College Press.

West, M. (2000) Cadre development, in D. Hopkins (2001) *School Improvement for Real*, London: RoutledgeFalmer.

West, M., Jackson, D., Harris, A. and Hopkins, D. (2000) Learning through leadership, leadership through learning, in K.A. Riley and K.S. Louis (eds) *Leadership for Change and School Reform*, London: RoutledgeFalmer.

Westoby, A. (ed.) (1988) *Culture and Power in Organisations*, Milton Keynes: Open University Press.

Willis, P. (1977) *Learning to Labour: How Working Class Kids Get Working Class Jobs*, Farnborough: Saxon House.

Willower, D. (1992) Educational administration: Intellectual trends, in R.L. Ebel (ed.) *Encylopedia of Educational Research*, 6th edn, Toronto: Macmillan.

Wolcott, H. (1977) *Teachers versus Technocrats*, Ann Arbor, MI: Centre for Education Policy Making, University of Oregon.

Woods, P. (1996) Beyond consumerism: The idea of consumer-citizenship, *Management in Education*, 10(3): 15–16.

Woods, P.A, Bennett, N., Harvey, J.A. and Wise, C. (2003) Understanding distributed leadership. Paper given at the British Educational Association annual conference, Edinburgh, September 2003.

Wragg, E.C., Haynes, G.S., Wragg, C.M. and Chamberlin, R.P. (2000) *Failing Teachers?* London: Routledge.

Index

academic attainment 2
action learning 142, 156
action research 142, 156
administrative social justice 10,
    159, 160, 161
advocacy 41, 46, 139
ages and stages of National
    Curriculum 105
alliances 140, 154
Allix, N.M. 34–5, 44, 72
allocation of teaching groups
    112
Alvesson, M. 87
ambiguity theory 5
Anderson, G.L. 70, 81, 123, 134
appraisal 143–4, 157
approval 39
assemblies, school 3
associative (affiliative) social
    justice 160, 161
attitudes 7–8
    influence of parents' attitudes
        on students 19–20
    students' 9–10
Aubrey, C. 32, 52, 70, 123, 133
authentic relationships 32, 114,
    124, 157
authority 8, 34, 35, 36–8
    delegated 37, 38, 39–41, 135,
        145
    middle leaders 39–42, 61, 145
autonomous learners 116

Bacharach, S. 10, 34, 35, 36, 37,
    133
Ball, S.J. 6, 17, 29, 31, 53, 57, 133
Barker, B. 12, 14, 17, 22, 23, 29,
    86, 136, 155
Beare, H. 84, 92
Beaty, L. 142
Begley, P.T. 6, 71, 80
behaviour 3, 9–10
    negotiation of rules of 117
behaviour policies 99–100
beliefs 93
Benjamin, S. 6, 7, 54, 68, 69, 96,
    111, 115
Bennett, N. 32, 34, 36, 53, 72, 134
Beresford, J. 2, 110, 116, 157
Bhabha, H. 89
Blase, J. 57, 70, 81, 122, 123, 134
Blau, P. 55–6
Blease, D. 23, 121
Bottery, M. 80, 122, 123
boundaries, organizational 2,
    19–20
Bourdieu, P. 9, 15, 36, 70, 101,
    107
Bowe, R. 17
Bradley, C. 46, 139
Brighouse, T. 14
bureaucracy 159, 160
bureaucratic micro-political
    strategies 58, 59
Burns, J.M. 5, 35, 38, 46